Relationship Agreements

A Simple and Effective Guide for Strengthening Communication, Reducing Conflict, and Increasing Intimacy to Design Your Ideal Relationship

Eri Kardos

Certified Integral Coach and Speaker

www.EriKardos.com

What Others Are Saying about Eri Kardos & Her Strategies

"Eri's bold new strategy really gets at the heart of what underlies frustrations in intimate relationships: difficulty with communication, trust, and honesty. Her approach, guided by insight and intuition, is smartly presented and something every relationship will benefit from."

–Fred Luskin, PhD
Director, Stanford Forgiveness Project;
Author, *Forgive for Love: The Missing Ingredient for a Healthy and Lasting Relationship*

"When you hear the phrase *relationship agreements*, you might think it means something difficult to create or that it focuses on enforcing rules. Eri Kardos shows us that it can be a way to deepen connection, get new clarity and perspective about your relationship, and offer an exciting opportunity to make something wonderful. Plus, she does it with genuine care, respect, and love. This is an incredibly useful book, whether you're just starting a relationship or you've been in one for decades."

–Charlie Glickman, PhD
Sexuality & Relationship Coach
www.MakeSexEasy.com

"This practical guide applies to all relationship types and can transform any relationship...from work to family to romance!"

–James Malinchak
Featured on ABC's Hit TV Show *Secret Millionaire*
Founder, www.MillionaireFreeBook.com

"Designing relationships is something I have been advocating for years with friends and clients, so when I saw Eri's book on Relationship Agreements, I was overjoyed. Agreements help couples build and rebuild a solid foundation of trust, intimacy, and connection, which then allows them to have the adventure, passion, and love they so desperately crave. This book is both practical and inspiring. Every couple needs to read this!"

–Natalie Vartanian
Life & Relationship Coach
Founder, www.SexThePodcast.com

"With her conversational yet respectful voice, Eri Kardos helps you navigate the murky waters of getting what you really want out of your relationships with her latest book, *Relationship Agreements*. Informative, easy to read, and engaging, *Relationship Agreements* lays out a road map that is accessible regardless of the stage of your relationship. Kardos effortlessly combines real-world testimonies from her clients, advice from experts, and perspective from her contributing author, Adam.

Whether you are starting anew, transitioning to a deeper intimacy in your current relationship, or discovering you want something more, *Relationship Agreements* will help you express, and achieve, your desires. Eri's book is just a facet of the excellence she has to offer."

–Rachel Bowen
Consent Academy Curriculum Developer & Writer

"The trouble with agreements is that we so often think we have them when we don't. Oops – we forgot to actually *talk* about them! I've been there, and I don't recommend it. Eri's book walks you through actually talking and deciding what they are. Helpful!"

–Betty Martin, DC
30-year Practitioner & Pioneer in the Nature of Touch
www.BettyMartin.org

"'Say what's not being said' is one of my relationship mantras, and Eri does a wonderful job sharing tools that will help you and your loved ones find the words and the courage to be the change you want to see in the bedroom and design your ideal relationship."

–Reid Mihalko
"America's Favorite Sex Geek"
Featured on *The Oprah Winfrey Network* and *Netflix*

"Eri's frame on relationship agreements is fresh, intimate, respectful, and genuinely helpful."

–Sarah Jones
Founder, Introverted Alpha
Featured in *Forbes & Cosmopolitan*

"Whether you were referred to her book by a friend, heard her on your favorite podcast, subscribe to her newsletter, or are learning about her for the first time – Eri's approach to relationships will give you a brand-new perspective on what a relationship CAN BE, and help you design the relationship you desire."

–Jolie Dawn
Best-selling Author, *Empowered, Sexy and Free*
#1 Selling Spirituality Book (Ranked with
The Alchemist & The Power of Now)

"Eri is an honest breath of fresh air in helping relationships grow with strong, positive communication and teaching people to co-create the relationship they desire."

–The Huffington Post

Dedication

This book is for all those who intentionally question the path they are told to walk, and then choose their own adventure.

For [erotically intelligent couples],
love is a vessel that contains
both security and adventure,
and commitment offers
one of the great luxuries of life: time.

Marriage is not the end of romance;
it is the beginning.

They know that they have years
in which to deepen their connection,
to experiment, to regress, and even to fail.

They see their relationship
as something alive and ongoing,
not a fait accompli.

It's a story that they are writing together,
one with many chapters,
and neither partner knows how it will end.

There's always a place they haven't gone yet,
always something about the other
still to be discovered...

—Esther Perel

Table of Contents

Introduction.. xv

How to Use This Book... xxi

Chapter 1: How a Relationship Agreement Will
Transform Your Relationship... 1
    Who Are Relationship Agreements for?...................... 1
    Meet "Fred" 3
    Choosing Your Own Path 5

Chapter 2: What Are Agreements? 13
    Rules vs. Agreements 13
    Time and Trust 16
    Living Document 18

Chapter 3: "Inquire Within" 27
    "Don't Ask, Don't Tell" or "Firehose"? 27
    "Inquire Within"...29
    Tips for "Inquiring Within" 32
    Jealousy 35

Chapter 4: Replacing Veto Power 41
    Veto Power and Trust 41
    Examples of Veto Power 43

Chapter 5: Navigating Conflict 49
    Rules of Engagement 49
    Timeout! 50
    Pre-Loaded Signal 50
    Cool-Down Time 51
    Self-Care during Cool-Down Period..........................52
    Tools for Reconnecting 53
    Dialoguing Tools 55

Chapter 6: Avoiding Unwanted Surprises 63
    What Constitutes a Surprise? 63
    Timing Is Everything.......................................64
    Be Realistic 67

Chapter 7: Check-Ins...73
    Channeling Our Emotions 73
    Let's Pause and Clarify....................................75
    Mitigating Fear 76
    Self-Care Prior to Check-In Time....................77

Chapter 8: Creating YOUR Relationship Agreement........83
    Where to Begin: Personal Work......................83
    The Staycation...84
    Help – I am Freaking Out or Feeling Resistant!........89
    Zen Reminders 90

Chapter 9: Samples to Get You Started 95
    First-Time Sample Staycation Schedule 96
    Sample Relationship Agreement Topics.................100

Chapter 10: We Did It! Now What?!....................113
    Make It Accessible..113
    Revisiting and Revising Your
    Relationship Agreements 114
    Sample Veteran Staycation Schedule 114
    Broken Agreements...115
    You Are Not Alone 116

Chapter 11: Application for Ethical Non-Monogamy......121
    How a Relationship Agreement Will
    Transform Your Relationship (Chapter 1)..............125
    "Inquire Within" (Chapter 3) 128
    Replacing Veto Power (Chapter 4) 131
    Avoiding Unwanted Surprises (Chapter 6) 132
    Check-Ins (Chapter 7)....................................134
    Creating YOUR Relationship Agreement
    (Chapter 8) 135

Conclusion 137

References and Suggested Further Reading 139

Gratitude 143

About the Contributing Author 145

About the Author 147

A Final Note: Is This Book Written for You? 149

Introduction

You just picked up a powerful relationship communication guide that has been in the making for several years. In this book are the keys to changing the way you approach your partnership. If you choose to embark on this adventure of creating a Relationship Agreement with your partner, you'll have a well-articulated physical expression that demonstrates how your relationship grows and changes with time, just like you!

What You Can Expect in This Book

This book will provide you and your partner a framework and the resources you will need to explore the idea of a Relationship Agreement. It will develop your understanding of the power this agreement holds in transforming your partnership. In addition, it will help you identify next steps and create your own physical expression of your bond.

From personal experience and from my work with clients, I can vouch for this guide as being applicable and powerful for:

- (Re)building trust
- Strengthening communication
- Navigating conflict
- Reducing assumptions and expectations
- Increasing intimacy

It is most helpful when:

- Building a new relationship foundation
- Preparing for marriage (and other big commitments)
- Allowing individuals and relationships to grow over time

- Getting "unstuck" when a relationship has stagnated
- Making a clear co-parenting plan
- Creating smoother transitions when a relationship is ending
- Opening a safer space for divorce and other potentially difficult conversations
- Fostering a friendship based on mutual understanding after the romance is gone

Meet Eri Kardos, Author

Hello! My name is Eri Kardos. I am an international speaker and relationship coach. I work with clients all over the globe, and I empower them to design their ideal relationships and lives.

My unique background in sexuality studies, human behavior, international business, and leadership development opened the door to working with a variety of people. After graduating from the world's #1 international business school, I discovered I could provide valuable insights to leaders of large corporations. As a human resources professional, I spent a lot of time coaching leaders on business strategy and human capital. Over time I developed relationships based on trust and earned credibility with many of these industry leaders. I began to learn about their lives outside of the office. They shared similar struggles and concerns about their relationships (or lack thereof). In many cases, the stress of these relationships had an impact on their ability to thrive at work and in other areas of life. I realized that there are many people who are successful in their careers but don't necessarily feel balanced and successful in their partnerships. I watched very talented, successful leaders across some of the most well-known companies grow in their careers but flounder in their romantic partnerships. It was a powerful experience to see how I could utilize tools and coaching to help them create sustainable and strong relationships in both.

By sharing relationship tools that I had gathered over the years, I helped these leaders achieve significant positive changes in happiness levels at work and at home as they applied these tools skillfully with my guidance. The positive changes in my clients' lives had me motivated and hungry for more tools to share. I decided to earn my integral coaching certification from New Ventures West, which led me to study in San Francisco and Copenhagen for a year. I pursued my passion and launched my own coaching business with my established clients from large companies including Amazon, Google, and Microsoft. Through many referrals my business quickly grew, and I am honored to say that I have positively impacted hundreds of couples and individuals around the globe.

Relationship Agreement Evolution

Through many years of helping numerous clients of diverse backgrounds, I have observed that a Relationship Agreement is the single tool that holistically brings together the most essential pieces of a relationship. It sheds light on the dark areas, allowing partners to design their ideal relationship. On a personal note, it was because I used this tool early in my relationship to create a strong foundation with my then-partner, Adam, that I was able to successfully navigate the wonderful, challenging, and sometimes murky waters of being partners, spouses, and now friends and co-parents.

I am a huge education geek – I love to learn new things with others and stretch my understanding of how we are told the world *should* work and instead create something that *works for us*. Learning new skills and testing them out is a continuous process of trial and error. Many of my clients' Relationship Agreements (and my own!) were born from errors made along the journey and the successes that came out of learning from those errors. This book shares these stories with a broader audience to empower people to connect and grow together (and sometimes apart) over time in a healthy, open manner.

Early on, when I was sharing Relationship Agreements as a tool with my coaching clients, it didn't always go smoothly. We would hit roadblocks, and I would seek out new resources or tools that would help us navigate them to take the partnership to the next level. As my clients created their first Relationship Agreements, it became evident that different partnerships called for different formats, lengths, writing styles, tools, and rhythms in revisiting and revising their Relationship Agreements. Working with people with diverse personalities and varying definitions of what a "successful" relationship means to them challenged me to expand my resources and create a powerful guide for helping them design their ideal partnership.

I remember those early days when I learned the most valuable lesson: always keep learning. I attended workshops and trainings all over the world, hired amazing coaches to work with me, and read every book on relationships and personal development that I could get my hands on. (One of my most prized possessions is my large library of books.) It is only after these many years of trial and error, finding the best fit path, and growing as a coach and relationship guide that I now share these Relationship Agreements with you.

Meet Adam Kardos, Contributing Author

Adam:

Hi! My name is Adam Kardos. I come from an IT background, which lends itself more to machinery and less to people. My jobs included keeping systems up and running smoothly, and making problems go away. What I discovered in my work is that my real passion is interacting with people – solving problems, getting to what is human and what is real. Thus, I joined Eri and trained to become a coach to gain skills in understanding how we work together. Along the way, I discovered more about myself and what is important to me. Eri and I are very different in how we approach life, in how we conduct personal affairs, in how we look at momentum and gain personal incentive, and in what drives us. Our Relationship Agreements allowed us to have a medium and a path forward together, making sure we understood each other at every stage, and if we didn't, exploring how we could make that better.

One of the amazing outcomes of reading and re-reading our Relationship Agreement was realizing the subconscious beliefs we held about what was the "right" way to do things, based on the stories and beliefs held by our parents, our culture, and our society, that came into our line of sight. We were able to look at these beliefs and ask ourselves, "Which of these do we want to subscribe to?" Through the process of writing things down, we discovered that some things made sense and held true for our relationships, while other pieces did not quite fit. Many messages we were taught growing up felt disingenuous and limiting. Much of our time was spent unraveling what was assumed from our default families of origin. Then came the even tougher question: if this is not what we want in our relationship, then what? Therein lies the good stuff...

How to Use This Book

This book will follow the flow I found to be most helpful when teaching workshops on Relationship Agreements. It is not necessary to read it straight through. Some chapter titles may speak to you more than others. I encourage you to read Chapter 1 first, then jump around in the sections that seem most relevant to you in Chapters 2-8. Once you have finished all those chapters, you can finish up with Chapters 9-11. This will give you a full perspective before creating your own Relationship Agreement.

It is important for me to recognize that there is great fluidity in the world, specifically in our relationship structures, in our sexuality, in our gender identity, and in our desires. This book is meant to serve as a tool for all people – regardless of these labels and identifiers. Throughout this book, I use the pronouns *he/his* and *she/her* simply because these have been the identities I have the most experience with. However, if you find other pronouns are more comfortable, I invite you to replace my language with one that is most authentic/relevant to you and your partner.

In a similar vein, I have found that the language and verbiage that people use when discussing their relationships can hold conflicting meaning. For example, one person might define *marriage* as a legal union between two people, whereas another person might define it as a spiritual state of union between people. I encourage you to be curious and open-minded to the use of different terms for relationship styles that my colleagues and I use throughout this book. If the term *marriage* is not something that you envision for your life, simply replace the word with one that fits better.

This book is written for *you*. I have applied these concepts and tools to relationship structures of all types with people from diverse cultures all around the globe. Whatever identifying labels you connect with (straight, gay, lesbian, transexual, queer, monogamous, polyamorous, swinger, open, etc.) and whatever cultural and religious values you hold, this book contains tools to navigate partnership challenges and help you design your ideal relationship.

Key Points

Along the way, I will highlight important phrases and key points that I think may stand out to you. You can find these pull quotes interspersed throughout the book in italics.

Resources

The end of the book is filled with resources I have collected over the years. Each one is special, and I encourage you to check them all out as you have time/desire.

What Other Experts Are Saying

It is often helpful to hear from other relationship experts when you are navigating new territory. Throughout this book I have included quotes and professional tips from my colleagues to give additional perspective and resources. You can find these located throughout the chapters in shaded boxes.

Example Dialogues and Situations

Apart from living through situations, hearing another person's experience may be the most powerful way to learn. I've scattered example dialogues and situational examples throughout the book to help you connect with real-life application. Each example actually happened to me, my colleagues, or to one of my clients. Names and personal information have been changed to protect the confidentiality of the people involved.

Take-Away Summaries

Want a quick refresher? Check out the summary at the end of each chapter!

Invitations

In my coaching practice, I invite my clients to do "homework" in between our sessions. This book will have similar types of invitations for you. Should you choose to accept, they will help you do the work needed to prepare for and create a meaningful Relationship Agreement. Please complete the invitations on your own. Once you and your partner have completed an invitation, please exchange your "aha" moments as it feels safe and appropriate to do so.

The invitations can be found at the end of each chapter. They will be separated into the three categories: Self-Reflection, Self-Observation, and Exercise. Within each category I created a structure to help you understand the *Intention, Implementation,* and *Instruction*.

Self-Reflections are journal exercises designed to increase your awareness and understanding of how you feel/think/ process/hear/understand your world. They will help expose patterns, explore depths, and add clarity and direction. I will give a detailed structure for each reflection, but just to give you a heads up, a general structure for these is to pause and reflect once daily, and then capture your thoughts in a journal. This should take around 15-20 minutes at the end of each day. If a specific self-reflection invitation stands out to you, I encourage you to repeat it daily for at least a week to see where the writing leads you.

Self-Observations are intended to help you pause and take note of your current way of being. Throughout your day as you encounter life and situations that apply to the self-observation, stop to reflect on the questions. Each observation exercise will come with an outlined structure. However, a general guide is to pause to reflect two times per day (roughly at mid-morning and after dinner). If a specific self-observation invitation stands out to you, I encourage you to repeat it daily for at least a week. Keep notes and begin to identify themes.

Exercises will include a variety of activities for you to explore. The intention for each is to prepare your body, mind, and heart for the work it takes to have a meaningful, authentic, and ever-growing relationship with yourself and your partner. These exercises will include wonderful resources including books, music, podcasts, articles, workshops, events, activities, and more. If a specific exercise invitation stands out to you, I encourage you to repeat it or look for similar resources.

It is important to note that each of these invitations is meant to take you below the surface of where you currently are, and yet they will not be able to take you to the depths of working directly with me as your coach. If you connect with my invitations and style of working, then I encourage you to check out my special private coaching invitations to you at the end of the book. I am happy to point you to more wonderful resources and explore the possibility of working together and empowering you to choose your own adventure in relationships and life.

1 How a Relationship Agreement Will Transform Your Relationship

Who Are Relationship Agreements for?

Relationship Agreements are for anyone who is currently in a relationship or wants to be in one. It does not matter if you are two months, two years, or two decades into your relationship. Creating your Relationship Agreements together can be transformational at all stages of connection. You also don't have to be in a romantic partnership right now to start thinking about your own values, who you are as an individual, what you want in a future relationship with someone, and how you partner with another person.

One of the tools I picked up along the way is to create a Personal Agreement for yourself. Think of it as a simple document outlining who you are in this moment, and what kind of partner you are looking for in life based on what you value. Think of it as a user manual about yourself! This is a helpful brainstorming tool to create before you make a Relationship Agreement with a partner, but not an essential step if you feel ready to launch into your Relationship Agreement now. In Chapter 8, I will talk more about the importance of self-development and self-awareness, and the incredible impact these can have on your relationships. To create your own Personal Agreement, check out Invitation 1.2 at the end of this chapter.

Most of the time, I teach people how to create a Relationship Agreement made between romantic partners. However, I have also found Relationship Agreements to be equally powerful when applied to a variety of other situations. The Relationship Agreement does not have to be with only one person – you could create one with multiple people, or you could have multiple Relationship Agreements with important people all across your life: perhaps with a work colleague, your spouse, former spouse, parent, child, or sibling. The basic idea is simple: you already have informal agreements with these people, but they are not necessarily verbalized or malleable, let alone written down to help keep everyone on the same page. Creating this document together reflects who each of you are in this relationship – at this moment – and has a built-in flexibility to adapt and change over time. It reduces assumptions and limits frustrations when you don't do things the way you always did them in the past. It allows you to understand your partner better and see the world through her eyes more clearly. It allows you to be agile and learn over time what you want in life and relationships. You are not the same person today that you were a year ago, so why not let your significant other know who you are now and learn who they have become?

Going through the process of designing your ideal relationship through co-creating a Relationship Agreement with your partner can be incredibly insightful. It can help you understand your partner in a way that you possibly did not before this moment. This sharing of perceptions, values, and beliefs opens you to new knowledge, greater truth, and deeper love, as Harville Hendrix (2008) explains.

What Other Experts Are Saying

"When you accept the limited nature of your own perceptions and become more receptive to the truth of your partner's perceptions, a whole world opens up to you. Instead of seeing your partner's differing views as a source of conflict, you realize that they are a source of knowledge: 'What are you seeing that I am not seeing?' 'What have you learned that I have yet to learn?' Relationships give you the opportunity to be continually schooled in your own reality and in the reality of another person. Every one of your interactions contains a grain of truth, a sliver of insight, a glimpse into your hiddenness and your wholeness. As you add to your growing fund of knowledge, you are creating reality love, a love based on the emerging truth of yourself and your partner, not on romantic illusion." (Hendrix, 2008, p. 135-136)

....

"Creating this document together reflects who each of you are in this relationship – at this moment – and has a built-in flexibility to adapt and change over time."

....

Throughout this book, I will focus on romantic partnerships. However, you can modify the big ideas in this book to fit the relationships you are creating agreements for, no matter what role the person plays in your life. This type of agreement and the types of conversations that can come out of it can be very helpful and healthy when navigating life's murky waters together.

Meet "Fred"

Adam:

A common misconception in conversations about relationships is the idea that there are only two unique entities to consider in a partnership: you and your significant other. We find that when a relationship is formed and the dynamic is engaging, a third entity comes into play: the shared space between you and your partner. Two of our married friends refer to this third entity (i.e., their relationship) as "Fred." They imagine Fred to be a furry blue monster about four feet in height.

∙∙∙

"We find that when a relationship is formed and the dynamic is engaging, a third entity comes into play: the shared space between you and your partner."

∙∙∙

Whenever these two are setting aside intentional time to work on their relationship (e.g., go on a date or take a vacation), they reference it as "taking Fred to the zoo" to remind themselves that they are investing in the relationship and not necessarily just in the individuals involved. This kind of abstraction from self challenges each partner to consider investing for the sake of the relationship and not for yourself; you are doing it for Fred.

This outlook lowers your risk of taking things personally. If you choose to go out of your way to do something sweet for your partner and she doesn't acknowledge, appreciate, or even notice the act, it is easy to take the situation very personally. However, when you are doing something for the sake of the relationship and your partner does not find it particularly helpful, it may still feel challenging, but it usually does not have the same hard edge as when it is done for the individual.

Eri:

One of my favorite things about the concept of "taking Fred to the zoo" is that it serves as a reminder that it's not just about me and it isn't just about my partner; it's actually about this thing we are creating and nurturing together. I can easily look down at a little fuzzy blue monster with compassion and forgiveness, and pour extra love into building, creating, and helping guide this little one through life, almost like a child. Relationships operate in a similar manner – they need extra feedings, they need extra care – they don't just function and survive on their own. Mainstream society tells us all you have to do is find your Prince/Princess Charming and the work is done. The effort goes into the hunt (i.e., dating), and once the hunt is done, so is the work. The reality is that finding your partner may be one of the easier things to do in life. Staying in partnership with your beloved and maintaining a healthy relationship where you both understand, respect, and love each other can be much more challenging. It can also be that much more rewarding!

. . . .

"The reality is that finding your partner may be one of the easier things to do in life. Staying in partnership with your beloved and maintaining a healthy relationship where you both understand, respect, and love each other can be much more challenging. It can also be that much more rewarding!"

. . . .

This approach is not something most of us are programmed to do by default; it's not something we were taught in school, and it's not something most parents or caregivers modeled well for us. The good news is now, as an aware adult, you have the opportunity to change how you operate – to question your upbringing, how you react to others, and what you bring into a relationship. This moment of intention is similar to the process of becoming a new parent. The choice is in front of you now: "Is the way I was raised what I want to give my child?"

Choosing Your Own Path

Creating conscious Relationship Agreements allows you to step back and decide for yourself: "Is this how I want to continue handling conflict? What about my approach to providing care for a sick partner? Is that how I want to show up in this relationship?" If not, and if you are ready to start creating lasting changes, your Relationship Agreement will be a very effective tool to help you modify your behaviors to align with your values as an adult.

In addition, you can partner with your significant other and *choose* how you both will approach your relationship by "caring and feeding" together. Remember, your beloved was likely brought up differently than you were. He has a unique perspective on how to have a healthy relationship based on the culture, media, time period, and values of his caregivers. Creating "Fred" together means sharing and questioning your stories of origin to jointly decide what you both value in a relationship.

Adam:

One additional benefit of mutually investing in "Fred" is that it helps create a sense of community in the space we share instead of continuing to support an isolationist perspective. People from the USA are often raised in an individualistic culture where we are taught that we are responsible for ourselves and only ourselves – and nothing greater. Collectivist cultures would disagree; what you choose to do with your own self has an impact on those around you. In this case, what you choose to do with yourself has an impact on "Fred" and your partner. This slight change in perspective may give you time to pause for thought before you act on a decision that could impact those around you.

Take-Away Summary

Relationship Agreements can be co-created for a variety of different scenarios, including with a work colleague, spouse, former spouse, parent, child, or sibling. In this book, I will focus on creating a Relationship Agreement for people who are currently in relationship – romantic or not – or who want to be in one. It is important to note that you *already have* agreements with many people in your life. My goal is to give you a tool that will help you articulate and align your agreements, reduce assumptions, and allow you the freedom to change over time. Creating conscious Relationship Agreements allows you to step back and decide for yourself what you *actually* want from this relationship and co-create it with your partner.

Remember, relationships require attention, intention, and care. When a relationship is formed and the dynamic is engaging, a third entity comes into play: the shared space between you and your partner. I refer to this space as "Fred."

Invitations (Homework)

❏ **1.1 Relationship Agreement Partnerships**
Self-Reflection

❏ **Intention:** To raise awareness of the many opportunities available for you to create a Relationship Agreement with different people; to begin exploring how removing assumptions and expectations with your partner, parent, child, or colleague could create less stress in your life

....

❏ **Implementation:** Who would it be helpful for you to create a Relationship Agreement with in your life? Which people do you often feel like you are having to "mind read" in order to maintain a relationship? Who do you think would be open to creating a Relationship Agreement with you? Who would have the most resistance and why? Where are there assumptions and undiscussed expectations that heavily influence your relationship with this person?

....

❏ **Instruction:** Pause, reflect, and journal for 5-7 minutes at the end of each day. Don't worry about grammar or editing. Allow whatever thoughts there are to flow onto the paper. Try not to stop writing until at least 5 minutes are up. I encourage you to repeat this journal reflection daily for one week. At the end of the week, reread your journal and look for moments of clarity, direction, depth, and pattern exposure.

....

❏ 1.2 Create Your Own Personal Agreement (a.k.a. "User Manual")
Exercise

❏ **Intention:** To pause and reflect on who you are NOW, with all of your life experiences, all of your quirks, all of your baggage, and all of your magic

....

❏ **Implementation:** What do you want in romance, sex, love, and partnership? Think of this as writing out a form of a "user manual" about yourself that you might decide to share with others in the future.

....

❏ **Instruction:** Pause to reflect using the following questions:
1. Family Background/History (include some of your quirks).
2. What do you value?
3. What do you find attractive in a partner?
4. What's your idea of a perfect date?
5. What do you *really* like (foods, habits, communication styles, pet names, certain romantic/sexual acts, etc.)?
6. What do you *really* dislike (foods, habits, communication styles, pet names, certain romantic/sexual acts, etc.)?
7. What makes you feel loved, seen, and cared for?
8. How do you like to show love and affection?
9. What other areas are important for you and your partner to know about each other?

....

❑ **Instruction:** Once daily, pause to reflect, and then capture your thoughts in a journal. This should take around 15-20 minutes at the end of each day. Continue this for two weeks.

....

❑ 1.3 Create Your "Fred"
Exercise

❑ **Intention:** To bring a sense of aliveness and third-entity presence to your relationship; to give it shape and have a shared vision of what you are caring for, nurturing, and protecting

....

❑ **Implementation:** It may feel silly at first, but work with your partner to imagine what this third entity created in the shared space between you both looks like. What physical characteristics stand out? How tall is it? What color? Texture? What does it wear? What will you both call it? One set of clients I work with keeps a hard-drawn portrait of their little one hanging on the dining room wall as a daily reminder of its importance. How can you keep your "Fred" present in your minds and hearts?

....

❑ **Instruction:** Set aside 10-20 minutes of your date time to answer the questions above. Do this one time, and then implement your ideas for how you can keep your "Fred" present in your minds and hearts on a regular basis.

....

2 What Are Agreements?

Rules vs. Agreements

Adam:

Let's talk about the differences between rules and agreements. When people hear us talk about *Relationship Agreements*, they often imagine a legally binding document; when one person makes a mistake and breaks a "rule," the other person is called to administer punishment for the offense – which often means ending the relationship. This is *NOT* the spirit of the Relationship Agreements we are inviting you to create.

There are some subtleties that play an important role in how we decide what we are willing to do, what we are "allowed" to do, and what the consequence of our actions might be within the context of our relationship. A *rule* can be seen as what is allowed or forbidden. It is a simple delineation. Rules are ordained by something or someone and are not to be broken. On the other hand, an *agreement* is a consensus reached after a proposal between two or more people is validated. You can think of this as the difference between a legal contract and a social contract.

. . . .

"An agreement is a consensus reached after a proposal between two or more people is validated."

. . . .

If you break a rule, it usually leads to nasty, punitive consequences. In many of the cases I have observed, when one partner breaks a rule, it leads to the other partner also breaking a rule out of resentment, hurt, or anger. This can develop into a vicious cycle of rule breaking. In agree-ments, there are no intrinsic punitive measures. If an agreement is broken, it is brought to the attention of the person who broke the agreement, and a solution is sought by looking at the situation together. Looking at the situation includes questioning why it happened in the first place and what tools and resources are currently in place to prevent breaking such agreements. More often than not, agreements are broken unintentionally. They are also frequently broken because they were either not created in the spirit of an agreement but forced into, or because one person no longer agrees to it anymore and a change in agreement is needed. Co-creating these agreements together and staying in communication about change requests can curtail the toxic cycle of rule breaking.

> *"More often than not, agreements are broken unintentionally."*

Eri:

It is important to remember that creating Relationship Agreements means that two or more independent, healthy, consenting individuals who have freedom of choice are joining forces to create something wonderful and unique together. This is not a parenting situation – this is your partner. Every morning, you have the choice to be in this relationship; you also have a choice to be in an abusive relationship, and you have a choice to be in a healthy relationship. Each day that you continue to invest in the relationship, you are making a conscious choice.

> *"Each day that you continue to invest in the relationship, you are making a conscious choice."*

These Relationship Agreements are a reflection of what you are committing to do to the best of your ability along with your partner. By committing to these agreements, you commit to upholding them until you decide it is time for a change. This is very different from when you were a child and might have been told: "Do this or else suffer the consequences." By agreeing to come together in this way, you're also agreeing to be responsible for adjustments and conversations when things don't go as smoothly as you had hoped. We are all human, and we inevitably mess up. The good news is we have the capacity to learn, grow, and better ourselves. We can work through our individual guilt and shame to make better choices for our future.

Most of the agreements we will be talking about in upcoming chapters reflect common patterns I have seen while working with hundreds of couples where they have made mistakes and hurt each other, intentionally or unintentionally. Through that pain, they learned new ways of being. They grew closer in this new state of being, and offered forgiveness for their chosen behaviors. This is a powerful and amazing byproduct of sharing agreements and committing to grow together in good times and in bad. The reality is that we are not the same people we were six months ago, or six years ago, and we will not be the same people sixty years from now. Partnering for life (or however long your season together may be) is about celebrating the journey, with all of its bumps and bruises.

. . . .

"The reality is that we are not the same people we were six months ago, or six years ago, and we will not be the same people sixty years from now. Partnering for life (or however long your season together may be) is about celebrating the journey, with all of its bumps and bruises."

. . . .

Time and Trust

Over the years of working on my own relationships and observing other relationships, I've noticed a similar correlation between time and trust. The more time you spend together with your partner, the greater your understanding of his behavior and the better you are at predicting how he will react to a situation. In the early stages of our relationship, the agreements Adam and I created were rigid and nit-picky. We did this to establish very clear boundaries because we didn't know each other very well. Fear of the unknown, fear of abandonment, and fear of being hurt led us to create agreements that provided clear data points that helped reassure us that we could indeed trust our new partner. I had no historical reference of how Adam would behave in certain situations. I didn't know if his natural response would be fight, flight, or freeze. I didn't know how he would respond to certain projects or jobs we might want to do around the house or with our careers. This information comes with time together and intimately knowing your partner on multiple levels.

Adam:

We set up "guardrail agreements" to help ensure a certain measure of safety because we were both driving this car together. We did not yet trust that if one person was in the driver's seat and took a corner too sharply, we would not go flying off a cliff. Thus, we opted to put a guardrail on the corner.

Eri:

For example, when we were first seeing each other, it was really important to me to have quiet time with Adam before we went to sleep. I made a request that we both be home and ready to connect with each other by 10:30. The intention behind the request was to share our day and talk about what was on our minds and in our hearts. Honoring this agreement gave me a sense of security and stability. Over time, I observed Adam's commitment to follow through. This continued behavior was an important part of helping me understand who he was and how he valued our time and connection. It helped me trust in *us*. Eventually, I no longer needed my nightly reconnection time, and we altered our agreement to give more flexibility for opportunities when either of us wanted to stay out late with friends, work later hours, or simply take personal time to be alone. Having established a firm foundation of trust, it was much easier for me to encourage him to go out and enjoy himself, while not feeling worried that he may be breaking an agreement or forgetting about our relationship.

If both partners follow through on what you commit to, your trust will deepen over time. On the other hand, you may discover your partner chooses not to follow through on your shared agreements. This is potentially a very clear red flag that you might want to get out of the relationship. If you can grow together by making commitments to shared agreements and follow through on them, then over time your need for rigid agreements will lessen and leave room for more flexibility and spontaneity. Five years into our relationship, our agreements no longer looked what once seemed like tight guardrails. Our written Relationship Agreements had evolved into our joyous and reassuring manifesto. With time, I learned to predict (with very good accuracy) what he liked to eat, how he liked to spend his free time, what areas of his life he felt most stressed about, and how he liked to receive love and support. These things you can truly learn only when you are investing in each other with your time, communication, and trust.

Based on our observations, this is a natural progression in most relationships. What I am positing is that Relationship Agreements bring you closer to these times of deep trust and understanding of your partner in a safer, smoother way than by "just winging it" and hoping for the best.

Living Document

If I were to use "business-speak," I would call our Relationship Agreements a *living document*. This is not a one-time-and-it's-done activity. It's an ongoing commitment to refresh and modify agreements as you change and grow along your journey together. Honoring the intention to let it live and learn with you is crucial to using the tool successfully. Let time pass, and allow trust to be established. Be prepared to stretch or compress whatever agreements/boundaries you create together as life warrants.

Adam:

When you are creating your Relationship Agreements, I hope you create untenable agreements. Create agreements that are too broad in scope, too limiting, too poorly or ambiguously worded. Let these things happen with great enthusiasm and vigor. Fall on your face a bit, just like you did when you were a kid. Those were well-earned bruises that resulted in a phenomenal awareness about what stays upright and what goes sideways. Through the process of testing your Relationship Agreements and discovering what actually works, you'll learn more about each other, yourself, and how to love more deeply and safely with your partner.

> *"Through the process of testing your Relationship Agreements and discovering what actually works, you'll learn more about each other, yourself, and how to love more deeply and safely with your partner."*

Eri:

The process of growing together through stretching (and sometimes contracting!) your Relationship Agreements can be transformational for both the relationship and the individuals.

Choosing to design your own ideal relationship means that you will often wander off-map into uncharted lands. It takes great courage and a sense of trust that whatever lies out there in the unknown is worth pursuing. The journey of creating Relationship Agreements together requires you to set realistic expectations about the process of calibrating your agreements. For some, it will be smooth, and for others there will be steep learning curves. You may take a wrong turn from time to time and end up discovering things you never imagined about yourself and your partner. Allow the process to be whatever your relationship calls for, and enjoy both the journey and the destination.

I appreciate how Franklin Veaux and Eve Rickert describe creating successful agreements together:

What Other Experts Are Saying

"Healthy agreements are those *that encourage moving in the direction of greatest courage...* The agreements that work most consistently are those that are rooted in compassion, encourage mutual respect and empowerment, leave it to our partners' judgement how to implement them, and have input from – apply equally to – everyone affected by them. These include principles like the following: Treat all others with kindness. Don't try to force relationships to be something they are not. Don't try to impose yourself on other people. Understand when things are Not About You. Understand that just because you feel bad, it doesn't necessarily mean someone else did something wrong. Know that your feelings sometimes lie to you. Own your own mess. Favor trust over rules... Here are some characteristics of successful relationship agreements:

- They seek to place controls on one's self, not one's partners.
- They offer a clear path to success.
- They are clear, specific, and limited in scope.
- They have a defined practical purpose.
- They do not seek to sweep problems under the rug.
- They have a sunset clause if they are meant to provide space for dealing with a problem.
- They aren't aimed at unspoken expectations.
- They are renegotiable.
- They do not disempower people.
- They do not legislate feelings."
(Veaux & Rickert, 2014, p. 237-239)

Take-Away Summary

What is the difference between a rule and an agreement? At the heart, a *rule* is ordained by something or someone and is either allowed or forbidden. Rules are and are not to be broken. An *agreement*, on the other hand, is a consensus reached after a proposal between two or more people is validated. Those who create agreements seek resolution together when either person realizes that an agreement was broken. These Relationship Agreements are meant to be created by two or more independent, healthy, consenting individuals who have freedom of choice and are joining forces to create something wonderful and unique together.

Want to understand your partner more fully and be able to predict her behavior better? Time together will help you establish greater understanding of trust between you both – especially through "guardrail" agreements. Intentionally co-creating agreements increases your chances of deepening trust than by "just winging it" and hoping for the best. It is also important to note that this is a living document – an ongoing commitment to refresh and modify agreements as you change and grow along your journey together.

Invitations (Homework)

❑   2.1 Hopes and Fears
Self-Reflection

❑ **Intention:** To bring greater awareness and understanding of what aspects excite or terrify you when you consider creating a Relationship Agreement of your own; to give voice to these responses and honor the fact that they exist instead of ignoring them

     •••

❑ **Implementation:** What are your hopes for creating your Relationship Agreement? What are your fears about creating one? What moment from your past does each fear remind you of ? What might help you feel safer in creating a Relationship Agreement with your partner?

     •••

❑ **Instruction:** Pause, reflect, and journal for 10-15 minutes at the end of each day. Don't worry about grammar or editing. Allow whatever thoughts there are to flow onto the paper. Try not to stop writing until at least 10 minutes are up. I encourage you to repeat this journal question daily for one week. At the end of the week, reread your journal and look for moments of clarity, direction, depth, and pattern exposure.

     •••

❑ 2.2 Rules and Punishments
Self-Observation

❑ **Intention:** To reflect on the major influences that have shaped your perception of rules and punishments; to bring the awareness from your head to your body; to separate the past from the present

....

❑ **Implementation:** When you think of rules and punishments, who comes to mind from your childhood? As you recall this person and these situations, be gentle with yourself. Where do you sense these emotions in your body? Are your shoulders tight? Is your throat closed? Your stomach in knots? Close your eyes and take slow, deep breaths, imagining the air circling and releasing tension in these areas. Now, imagine your beloved. Remember that this person you are choosing to be with is not the original person you imagined. He may have characteristics that remind you of your parent/caregiver/teacher, but he is not that person. You are now an adult and get to choose wisely who you invest in and how you operate as consenting, strong individuals.

....

❑ **Instruction:** Take time for the self-observation by reflecting one time per day (roughly at mid-morning or after dinner). Keep notes and begin to identify themes. I encourage you to repeat this time of self-observation daily for one week. At the end of the week, reread your notes and look for moments of clarity, direction, depth, and pattern exposure.

....

❑ **2.3 Guardrail Agreements**
Self-Reflection

❑ **Intention:** To increase your awareness and understanding of how you feel/think/process/hear/understand your needs and values; to create space to ask for what you need to feel safe and trusting in this relationship, free from judgement

....

❑ **Implementation:** What kinds of "guardrail agreements" would you like to request to help you (re) establish a sense of trust in your partner? What would help you feel safe, seen, and loved? Do you have a sense of how long you would like this request to be honored? What underlying fear does this help assuage? What value does it help support?

....

❑ **Instruction:** Pause, reflect, and journal for 10-15 minutes at the end of each day. Don't worry about grammar or editing. Allow whatever thoughts there are to flow onto the paper. Try not to stop writing until at least 10 minutes are up. I encourage you to repeat this journal question daily for one week. At the end of the week, reread your journal and look for moments of clarity, direction, depth, and pattern exposure.

....

❑ 2.4 Time and Trust
Self-Reflection

❑ **Intention:** To set aside time for reflection about how people change over time; to honor the journey of change you have experienced

···

❑ **Implementation:** How has my trust in my partner changed over time as I came to know her better? What contributed to an increase or decrease of trust? How have I grown and changed over time? Who was I when I began dating, and who am I now? What can I do to instill more trust in our relationship?

···

❑ **Instruction:** Pause, reflect, and journal for 10-15 minutes at the end of each day. Don't worry about grammar or editing. Allow whatever thoughts there are to flow onto the paper. Try not to stop writing until at least 10 minutes are up. I encourage you to repeat this journal question daily for one week. At the end of the week, reread your journal and look for moments of clarity, direction, depth, and pattern exposure.

···

3 "Inquire Within"

"Don't Ask, Don't Tell" or "Firehose"?

In my work, I have seen two primary options for how emotionally charged subjects, such as previous or current partners, are discussed. The first is "Don't Ask, Don't Tell" (DADT). In this model, whatever happened is in the past, is none of anybody's business, isn't worth bringing up, and will not be discussed. The second is the "Firehose Method"; this is full disclosure wherein one partner divulges all the details of an event that happened, at every point, and on every level. This may be more information than is desired or requested.

These forms of communication are often used with any sensitive subject – not just sexual/intimate ones. Other types of situations may include potentially loaded topics such as:

- What you did on your girls' night out if your partner has strong feelings about being left out
- How much income you make and how you choose to spend your money
- The level of closeness and insider information you share with your best friend
- Your past traumatic experiences
- How you spent your 21st birthday if your partner has a hard time hearing about alcohol
- When you need to share an embarrassing or sensitive situation – and if you want to receive advice or simply be heard
- When you are going out for coffee with someone your partner does not speak to/engage with

....

*"I have seen two primary options for how emotionally
charged subjects, such as previous or current partners,
are discussed:... 'Don't Ask, Don't Tell' or the
'Firehose Method'... Many of my clients wanted
another option, so I invite you to try a new method that
I call 'Inquire Within.'"*

....

Both of these methods tend to trigger feelings of unease
in one or both partners over time. In the first method, the
old saying of "ignorance is bliss" may create a false sense of
security. However, at some point you will learn something
about your partner's past, or you will find evidence that will
shatter the rosy image you hold of your partner. Often times it
can trigger "retroactive jealousy" about the experiences they
shared with others (i.e., *not you*) in the past. Once this bubble
of false security is popped, it is often difficult to go back to the
envisioned utopia. This is when I see clients begin to question
their own sense of safety in the relationships.

In the second method, both partners commit to sharing
ALL the details of life, especially regarding potentially triggering
situations. For example, if you ask your partner about his former
lovers, he would be committed to sharing all of the nitty-gritty
details from emotional depth of connection to graphic sexual
detail. Often times, this is far more information than what
receivers want to hear. Perhaps they are really interested in the
emotional connection but prefer not to know about the physical
play-by-play. I find that many people ask/demand full
disclosure because they are uncomfortable with the unknown,
even though it can lead to receiving more information than they
can handle. Being able to tolerate the discomfort takes practice
and a different option than what the "Firehose Method" offers.

Using this technique usually leads people to question their own sense of safety in the relationship.

"Inquire Within"

Many of my clients wanted another option, so I invite you to try a new method that I call "Inquire Within." The name of this technique came about when I was helping someone process the internal dialogue he was having around his desires to know some of the details but not all of them. He explained to me that many times the information that he cared about was different from what his partner tended to naturally share, or the rate at which the information flowed was overwhelming for him. It was not a matter of trust, but a matter of him having the power to check in with himself and be honest about the type of information he was prepared to hear, at a pace he was comfortable receiving.

"Inquire Within" is when receivers control the flow of information, have checkpoints along the way, and ensure they are getting only the information they want. An opportunity to "Inquire Within" could happen at any time. It might happen when one partner asks about a past emotional or physical experience. This could be with platonic friends or prior partners (see bulleted examples listed above). Another situation might arise where one partner has the opportunity to meet up with a former lover to share coffee. Or perhaps, one partner is experiencing feelings and starting to fantasize about someone she works with, was introduced to, or even met on the street. The partner doesn't necessarily want to act on these feelings, but wants to share the experience openly and process her curiosity with her trusted partner. This tool can be incredibly useful for strengthening your communication as you design your ideal relationship built on trust, vulnerability, and authenticity.

....

"'Inquire Within' is when receivers control the flow of information, have checkpoints along the way, and ensure they are getting only the information they want... This tool can be incredibly useful for strengthening your communication as you design your ideal relationship built on trust, vulnerability, and authenticity."

....

An example might be something akin to talking about a past lover. Your partner may be curious about what happened between you both. Using "Inquire Within," a gradual discussion is safely unfurled, where sensitive subjects can be addressed intently without feeling as though too much or not enough information is being shared.

....

"'Inquire Within' unfurls a gradual, safe discussion, and sensitive subjects can be addressed intently, without feeling as though too much or not enough information is being shared."

....

Let's run through an example:

Josh:　　"Hey, I keep hearing you talk about this old relationship you had with Miguel. What was that relationship like?"

Emily:　"Thanks for asking. It was a really significant relationship in my life, and I do think about how much I grew from that relationship. I'm not quite sure what aspect you'd like to hear about, though."

Josh: "Right now, I'm curious about the sexual connection that you both shared. It sounds like it might have been really intense, the way I've heard some of the anecdotes in the past. Would you mind going into a little more detail about that? I'm feeling a little uncomfortable, and I feel perhaps if I had a little more context, it might not seem so scary to me."

Emily: "Sure! Miguel was my first partner, and I lost my virginity to him. So, I think that made a big impact on me in terms of learning more about my body and how I connect with people. I think no matter who my first partner was, that would have left an impression. In my case with Miguel, I really learned about the gift of receiving pleasure and what it meant to be taken care of. We spent much of our intimate time performing and receiving oral sex, specifically just being very exploratory in that area."

Josh: "Ok. It sounds like the intensity I've heard you speak with regarding Miguel was around the emotional context of a first experience and the exploratory relationship that you guys shared. I think I have a little more solace and clarity around that subject now. I feel better about it – thanks for explaining!"

Emily: "Thank you for asking."

Notice in this example dialogue how the receiver (Josh) controlled the flow of information and how the sender (Emily) was careful to stop after covering a main point. If you were to observe the dialogue in action, it might have small pauses after each question is answered. During this pause, the receiver is checking in with himself and noticing how his emotions and body are responding. If he feels like he has reached the limit for how much he can take in at this time, he will stop asking questions and thank the sender for sharing.

This conversation often works best when both partners have time and patience for each other. I invite receivers to be gentle and tune into their heart. What do you *really* want to know? Are you ready to process whatever information you hear? If not, how are you prepared to inquire more at a later time instead of pushing past your comfort zone now? I also invite the sender to temper a desire to share everything or hide what is uncomfortable to talk about.

"Inquire Within" does *not* mean that the person sharing the information has the right to omit pertinent information if the leading person does not ask the right question. Prior to using this tool, make an agreement that the person sharing will quickly volunteer any information that may be crucial to the health and safety of the receiver. This will ease many worrisome thoughts and reduce unwanted surprises.

Tips for "Inquiring Within"

If you are new to the concept of sharing open, honest dialogue about situations that our mainstream culture often runs from, have no fear! With practice, this technique can change your relationship and how you connect with others in the world. It takes courage and great self-understanding to be on both the sending and receiving side of this dialogue.

Initiating "Inquire Within"

- Complete any preparation you need to have for this conversation. This may include reflecting about the situation, your feelings, what this brings up for you, what you might like to know in detail, what you are not prepared to hear at this time, and any requests you may like to make.

- As you make the request for a check-in, do so with a gentle approach that John Gottman and Nan Silver refer to as a "softened startup" (2000, p. 161). This technique will also be crucial for beginning any conflict dialogue tools. (See Chapter 5.)

What Other Experts Are Saying

"Softening the startup is crucial to resolving conflicts because, my research finds, *discussions invariably end on the same note they begin*. That's why 96 percent of the time I can predict the fate of a conflict discussion in the first three minutes! If you start an argument harshly – meaning you attack your spouse – you'll end up with at least as much tension as you began. But if you use a softened startup – meaning you complain but don't criticize or otherwise attack your spouse – the discussion is likely to be productive. And if most arguments start softly, your marriage is likely to be stable and happy... It's just a fact that people can change only if they are basically liked and accepted as they are. When people feel criticized, disliked, and unappreciated, they are unable to change. Instead, they feel under siege and dig in to protect themselves." (Gottman & Silver, 2000, p. 149; 161)

Now that you have been reminded of the importance of initiating the dialogue in an intentional and soft manner, let's look at tips for how to actually go through this crucial conversation with your partner.

Navigating the Conversation:

- Stay present with your partner.
- Notice how you are responding emotionally and physically.

- Create and maintain a safe space for your partner to speak/listen to you by regulating how intense your emotions may come across.
- At any point in time in the future, the person wanting to know more about the situation can ask. This is not a "you have 10 minutes to ask me whatever you want" game. Instead, he should feel safe asking for what he is prepared to hear the answer to when he is actually ready and without pressure.

Receiving Information (Flow Control):

- Ask only what you are ready to hear the answer to, even if that means waiting to ask the question until another time.
- Remember that your partner is courageously sharing because he trusts the safe space and your ability to ask for what you are ready to hear, even if it is painful or hard to hear.

Sending Information:

- Share information in "chapter stops" (i.e., big topic titles, where the receiver can decide to dig deeper or feel good knowing the big picture).
- Use *I* language as opposed to *you* language. For example: "I feel really angry when you are late for our date night" as opposed to: "You make me feel angry when you are late for our date night."
- Remember that your partner is asking because she is ready to hear the answer, even if it is painful or hard to hear.
- Be careful not to confuse your partner for your parental figures. She is not interrogating you to identify your crimes and punish you. She wants to *know you* and *understand you* more.

Jealousy

Jealousy is a topic that often comes up with my clients, especially as they use "Inquire Within." It is a complex and complicated mix of emotions ranging from fear, betrayal, loneliness, depression, anxiety, fear of loss/rejection, or fear of inadequacy. And as Christopher Ryan & Cacilda Jethá point out, experiencing jealousy is often rooted in our fears.

What Other Experts Are Saying

"So is jealousy natural? It depends. Fear is certainly natural, and like any other kind of insecurity, jealousy is an expression of fear." (Ryan & Jethá, 2010, p. 147)

For most people, exploring the feeling of jealousy is uncomfortable, and we seek to squash it immediately. It might help to reframe your perception of what jealousy is and how it can be useful for us. In her book *Love in Abundance: A Counselor's Advice on Open Relationships* (2010), Kathy Labriola creates a fantastic analogy for understanding jealousy and how we can use it as a helpful tool:

What Other Experts Are Saying

"I have come to believe that jealousy is a normal, natural response that serves a valid purpose. It comes up when we feel threatened with loss of something precious to us, and alerts us to pay attention to our relationships to make sure they are safe and sound.

Like a smoke alarm that may go off when you only burned the toast, jealousy may sometimes be an overreaction. When the smoke alarm goes off, it makes you pay attention. Once you are sure the problem is only burned toast and the house is not on fire, you can relax and forget about it. However, if the house is on fire, or your relationship is in danger, you can take whatever steps are needed to strengthen your relationship and fix whatever is causing the problem." (Labriola, 2010, p. 72-73)

I encourage you to actually stay with the feeling of jealousy instead of running from it or ignoring it. There are many resources on the topic of jealousy, and I included several of them in the resources sections at the end of the book. If you are someone who experiences jealousy, here are four tips taken from Tristan Taormino's book *Opening Up* (2008) to help guide you as you begin to explore this complex mix of emotions:

What Other Experts Are Saying

1. "The first step is to *let yourself feel jealous*. Even if you know, intellectually, that your emotion is irrational, you can still experience jealousy as real, visceral, and overwhelming. So let yourself feel it – validate and own the feeling. Don't criticize yourself or pile shame and judgement on top of it – that will just make you feel worse. Remember, too, that jealousy can be a learned reaction, one we see represented and reinforced all around us. Remind yourself that you may be reacting unconsciously in a way you think you should react.

2. When you feel any kind of jealousy, first ask yourself what's underneath the feeling. Do you feel left out, possessive, envious? Are you comparing yourself to someone else? Do you feel threatened, disrespected, angry? Did something specific happen to trigger your jealousy?

Remember that we often can't predict whether something will bother us until it happens and we get upset.

3. Seek support from friends, family or a therapist. Your
support system will help you assess the reality of the
situation as well as any suspicions or fears you may have.

4. Figure out what you need to feel better; it may be time to
yourself, reassurance from your partner, or a commitment
for some quality time." (Taormino, 2008, p. 162-163)

As Taormino explains, outside support and self-care are both
crucial components for processing these strong emotions and
learning how to manage them in mature, healthy ways. Learning
to understand the root of our emotions and the messages they
bring can actually lead us out of the discomfort and into a more
fulfilled and peaceful place. For more expert thoughts on the
power of acknowledging our emotions and using them as helpful
tools in our relationships, please see Chapter 7.

Take-Away Summary

I invite you to wander off the beaten path and try using "Inquire Within" as opposed to "Don't Ask, Don't Tell" or the "Firehose Method." In this new technique, the receivers control the flow of information, have checkpoints along the way, and ensure that they are getting only the information they want. Each person is responsible for their own behavior and emotions in the sender and receiver roles. Remember that an opportunity to "Inquire Within" could happen at any time and that "Inquiring Within" does *not* mean that the person sharing the information has the right to omit pertinent information if the leading person does not ask the right question.

Invitations (Homework)

❏ **3.1 Recognizing Unease and Using "Inquire Within"**
Self-Observation

> ❏ **Intention:** To help you pause and take note of your current way of being and both the physical and behavioral patterns you hold; these observations will prepare your body, mind, and heart for the work it takes to have a meaningful, authentic, and ever-growing relationship with yourself and your partner
>
> ·
>
> ❏ **Implementation:** What situations (real or hypothetical) make you feel uneasy to discuss or listen to? How do these feelings manifest in your body? What are they trying to tell you? How can you apply these observations when you and your partner use "Inquire Within"?
>
> ·
>
> ❏ **Instruction:** Throughout your day, as you encounter life and situations that apply to the self-observation, stop to reflect on the questions. Pause to reflect two times per day (roughly at mid-morning and after dinner). Keep notes and begin to identify themes. I encourage you to repeat this time of self-observation daily for one week. At the end of the week, reread your notes and look for moments of clarity, direction, depth, and pattern exposure.
>
> ·

❑   3.2 "Inquire Within"
Exercise

❑ **Intention:** To apply the cognitive learning tool in daily life and make it more accessible in your relationship

··

❑ **Implementation:** Practice using "Inquire Within" with your partner. Begin with an easier topic to start, such as: "How was your day?" After you understand the flow, discuss what worked and what was challenging. When ready, practice using a past situation that is more challenging to talk about. Once you have practiced this technique a few times in these controlled settings, try applying it to new situations that arise.

··

❑ **Instruction:** Set aside 20 minutes for easier topics and 60 minutes for more challenging topics to complete the exercise. Have one person lead the "Inquire Within," and then switch roles. Debrief on what went well and what might work better in the future.

··

4. Replacing Veto Power

Veto Power and Trust

One of the larger topics that comes up repeatedly during my discussions about creating Relationship Agreements is "veto power" and how it corresponds to trust in a relationship. Veto power is choosing to give your partner the ability to stop you from seeing someone or doing a specific activity that they believe is not good for you or the relationship (and vice versa). Couched under agreements is the idea of things being consensual. Veto flies in the face of this and implies ownership over the relationship. I find this to be ultimately destructive, not only for each partner's ability to make their own choices and feel empowered in how they choose to relate to the world, but also because it often fractures the trust you have built in your current partnership.

Building your relationship on a foundation of trust fortifies the structure over time. I invite you to act from a place of loving trust and have confidence in your partner's ability to make decisions that protect and nurture the relationship. While veto power might feel good in the beginning of a relationship, I invite you to think about this carefully – the ramifications can have lasting effects and build resentment. That being said, I do not believe that there is one "right way" of doing things – hence the power that comes from creating your own Relationship Agreement! In the same vein, there are some relationships wherein veto power works. If you are currently using veto power, I encourage you to view this chapter as an invitation to try another way of being. If it doesn't work for you, no worries! *Remember, YOU get to choose what works best for your relationship.*

....

"Building your relationship on a foundation of trust fortifies the structure over time. I invite you to act from a place of loving trust and have confidence in your partner's ability to make decisions that protect and nurture the relationship."

....

What Other Experts Are Saying

"When it comes to trusting in your partner, you are going to need to take a serious look at yourself first, and no we are not talking about trusting in yourself either. What you need to keep in mind when it comes to trust issues is that they often become a problem because it is some kind of issue you are secretly struggling with. For example, if you are worried about your partner cheating on you, it could be related to the fact that you have had thoughts about cheating on them. Finding out why you are having the trust issues can help you open up, but can also stop crazy thoughts racing through your head." (Riley, 2014, p. 43)

As Riley discusses, we often have concerns about what a partner *might* do to break our trust, which is rooted in our own fears, struggles, and insecurities. Before you rush in to control your partner's behavior, I invite you to spend time first exploring your own motives and emotions. Often times openly sharing your internal process creates space for more peace and less worry in your life.

Examples of Veto Power

Here's one example of when you might feel you would like
to have veto power: Your partner hangs out with a group of
friends you do not particularly like. Perhaps these friends use
language or engage in activities that don't resonate with you.
You feel like your partner might be picking up some bad habits
or spending a lot of quality time with them that she might
spend with you. You would like to be able to veto these friends.
In lieu of veto, you can courageously bring forward your
concerns with compassion and insight. You can discuss your
anxiousness about who your partner is hanging out with or
what she is engaging in – things you might feel she is missing
or not paying attention to.

*"In lieu of veto, you can courageously bring forward
your concerns with compassion and insight."*

Here's another example: Your partner is invited to catch up
with a former lover over a drink. You are concerned about the
emotional burden this person/situation may place on your partner
and on your relationship. You would like to veto this interaction.
Instead, you could let your partner know you're worried about
past stress being brought forward into the current situation, and
that you are experiencing your own fear of abandonment and
jealousy. You ask him to consider catching up in a different manner
(over the phone?), at another venue (over coffee instead of at a
bar?), or not at all.

One final example: Your partner has a habit of smoking
cigarettes, and you do not approve of this choice. You are
tempted to give her an ultimatum: either the cigarettes go,
or I go. This is another form of veto power and strips her of
the ability to choose for herself. Instead of vetoing an activity
that she connects with, you can choose to share your concerns

around why you would prefer she doesn't engage in this activity, including your own experiences (if applicable) with it in the past. I encourage you to share the emotions connected with your concerns during this dialogue. For example, you might share that you are feeling scared about her long-term health and fear losing her to cancer. You could request holding each other accountable for taking care of your bodies, letting her know that this concern comes from a place of care and love.

After expressing your concern, give your partner time and space to ruminate and do some self-reflection. If you are the one receiving difficult feedback, I invite you to listen as openly as possible, knowing that your partner cares for you and is feeling concerned. Thank him for being courageous in bringing this to you. In the end, it is up to each of you as individuals to act in a manner that you feel is best for yourself and for your relationship. In some cases, we choose partners who cannot make healthy decisions for themselves or for your shared relationship. If this is the case, observing the decisions they make over time can give you concrete examples about their (in)ability to establish trust in your relationship. If your partner is unable to make healthy decisions that honor your partnership, it may be time to transition to a friendship or end the relationship completely. It takes as much courage to end an unhealthy relationship as it does to partner through the difficult times in a healthy one.

....

"If your partner is unable to make healthy decisions that honor your partnership, it may be time to transition to a friendship or end the relationship completely. It takes as much courage to end an unhealthy relationship as it does to partner through the difficult times in a healthy one."

....

Take-Away Summary

Veto power is choosing to give your partner the ability to stop you from seeing someone or doing a specific activity that he believes is not good for you or the relationship (and vice versa). The big downside is that this power removes each partner's ability to make their own choices and feel empowered in how they choose to relate to the world, and can fracture the trust you have built in your current partnership.

Instead of using veto power, I invite you to replace it with a dialogue where you clearly, compassionately express your concern to your partner. Create space for your partner to process what she heard. If you are the one receiving the difficult feedback, remember that your partner values you and your relationship, which is why he is bringing it up. Try to hold gratitude for the courage it took your partner to share these concerns with you. At the end of the day, it is up to each of you as individuals to act in a manner that you feel is best for yourself and for your relationship.

Invitations (Homework)

☐ ## 4.1 Replace Veto Power
Exercise

☐ **Intention:** To apply the cognitive learning tool in daily life and make it more accessible in your relationship

. . . .

☐ **Implementation:** Create hypothetical situations where you and/or your partner would feel a desire to use veto power. Instead of doing so, practice the steps discussed in this chapter to talk through your concerns. Pay attention to how your body reacts at the start of the conversation, throughout the dialogue, and after the conversation has ended. Try to "hold space" for your partner by using active listening and truly hearing the unease. Remember that this is not a demand, simply a statement of concern and a request to have his feelings and thoughts considered before action is taken.

. . . .

☐ **Instruction:** Set aside 20 minutes for easier topics and 60 minutes for more challenging topics to complete the exercise. Have one person lead a dialogue where you may be tempted to use veto power, and then switch roles. It may be helpful to practice using a less triggering hypothetical situation before moving on to a more challenging one. Debrief on what went well and what would work better in the future.

. . . .

❑ 4.2 How Does My Body Respond?
Self-Observation

❑ **Intention:** To help you pause and reflect on your current way of being and both the physical and behavioral patterns you hold

....

❑ **Implementation:** As you practice these dialogues from Exercise 4.1, pause and take note of your responses. How does your body react? Do you want to fight, freeze, or flee the conversation? Where do you feel it in your body? What does this situation remind you of from your past? Try not to judge whatever feelings/thoughts come up for you. Simply take note and reflect on them, noticing if they hold a deeper message for you about your fears or values. If it feels safe, please share these observations with your partner.

....

❑ **Instruction:** Pause throughout exercise 4.1 and again after to reflect on your somatic (physical/body) experience of using this tool. Keep reflection notes afterwards and begin to identify themes. After you have completed the exercise three times, reread your notes and look for moments of clarity, direction, depth, and pattern exposure.

....

5 Navigating Conflict

Rules of Engagement

We all fight. In one way or another, things will come up, and there will be conflict. As my counselor, Tricia, once said, "No one is better at pushing your buttons than your significant other. It's their job." How we engage with conflict or run from it can be telling of how the relationship will progress. I like to call these "Rules of Engagement." Most of us don't have great examples of how to handle conflict. Nor were we taught healthy ways of experiencing and expressing difficult emotions and how to handle them productively as we navigate conflict.

Pause for a moment and reflect on how your parents and caregivers handled conflict when you were growing up. For most of us, they did not handle it well, and we don't particularly desire to emulate their approaches. However, it's often difficult *not* to emulate their poor conflict resolution behavior when blood pressures begin to boil. Imagine you are coming to the battlefield without any tools in hand, as is your partner. Yet you both expect to "win" the fight and defeat the other person. Odd how that works, isn't it?

What if you *both* start on equal footing when conflict arises, with tools that have been proven to work effectively so that you both can win and grow together? I want to share a few tips and tricks that can help you and your beloved in times of conflict.

....

*"What if you both start on equal footing when conflict
arises, with tools that have been proven to work effectively
so that you both can win and grow together?"*

....

Timeout!

When blood pressures begin to rise and tension between us
increases, try calling for a "timeout." It doesn't matter who
calls the timeout. What really matters is that someone notices
the rising tension that could lead to a big fight. A difference in
opinion is understandable. I don't use this tool for small arguments like where we will go to dinner. Instead, I reserve this for
when a situation comes up that has the potential to explode
soon from emotional capacity nearing its boiling point.

Pre-Loaded Signal

I suggest that you and your partner create a pre-loaded signal
to initiate the timeout. No, I am not talking about flipping your
partner off, though you may feel like it in the moment. This is an
activity to do together *before* you are nearing your next conflict.
Brainstorm a hand signal or a verbal safeword that will get your
partner's attention when emotions are elevated. I've seen people
use anything from a heart shape with their hands to choosing
obscure words like "flugelhorn." A simple one I have used was to
make what looks like a timeout sign using both of our hands in
the shape of a big letter "T" (often used in sporting events).

....

*"Brainstorm a hand signal or a verbal safeword that will
get your partner's attention when emotions are elevated.
I've seen people use anything from a heart shape with
their hands to choosing obscure words like 'flugelhorn.'"*

....

Once you have chosen a signal, it is time to "pre-load" it with important messages that resonate with both you and your partner. These statements are crucial for us to move forward safely in the relationship, but may be difficult to share in the heat of the moment.

One of my pre-loaded hand signals for timeout means: "I am noticing that we are starting to fight, and I want to call a timeout before this gets too heated and we say hurtful things without thinking. I love you, and I'm coming back to the conversation at a later time, a minimum of 30 minutes from now. I commit to not discussing this topic with you during that time." The pre-loaded statements that you co-create are in direct correlation with our fears of being abandoned, being unloved, and having unresolved conflict. Instead of having to fight harder and wrestle with your fight-orflight response, simply use your pre-loaded signal and take a minimum of 30 minutes apart.

· ·

"The pre-loaded statements that you co-create are in direct correlation with our fears of being abandoned, being unloved, and having unresolved conflict."

· ·

Cool-Down Time

Why 30 minutes apart? This is part of our biological response to threat. It takes a minimum of 30 minutes for the fight/flight/freeze chemical cocktail (i.e., adrenaline, norepinephrine, and cortisol) to flush from your body. During the first 30 minutes, you are in survival mode and behave more like a primate and less like a developed human. Thus, you and your partner have wonderful biological reasons to take some time and space to yourself when tensions rise if you both want to survive.

....

"You and your partner have wonderful biological reasons to take some time and space to yourself when tensions rise if you both want to survive."

....

Self-Care during Cool-Down Period

During your time apart, I suggest you each turn your attention to caring for yourselves through a series of introspective questions. A helpful acronym often referenced in 12-step programs is H.A.L.T. or "Hungry. Angry. Lonely (or Loaded). Tired." I use this as my checklist to walk through my current state.

H – Hungry: Do I have low blood sugar? When was the last time I ate something nutritious?

A – Angry: What is my emotional state? Did something happen earlier in my day that may be affecting me now? (E.g., did I get into a fight with my boss at work? Did my cat get sick?) Perhaps the situation we are fighting about is not *actually* what is causing the tension.

L – Lonely/Loaded: Am I feeling lonely and in need of attention, even negative attention? Am I under the influence of any substances that prevent me from resolving conflict in a sober manner?

T – Tired: Does my body need rest? Did I sleep well last night? If not, perhaps a 20-30-minute power nap is in order.

One other question I have my clients ask themselves comes from Dr. Frederic Luskin's book, *Forgive for Love* (2007). Pause and ask yourself if you are upset with your partner because of your own "unenforceable rules." These are any expectations or demands that you make of yourself, others, or life that you have no power to control. It's easy to get mad when we hold onto assumptions and expectations.

What Other Experts Are Saying

"How often and how deeply we get upset with our lovers depends on the kinds of relationship rules we have set up. When you have too many unenforceable rules or try too hard to enforce workable rules, you create stress. When you try to enforce a rule that is under your control, your life goes smoothly. Remember: there are rules you can enforce and those that you cannot... Nearly all relationship problems begin when our partners break an unenforceable rule. Our frustrated attempt to enforce such a rule is at the root of your anger toward your loved one. Feelings of anger, helplessness, or depression are all indications that you are trying to enforce something that cannot be enforced. Your anger is telling you that things are not working out the way you want them to. These situations are painful because you are not able to control them, even though you try over and over again to do so... Real love can emerge only when there is a choice." (Luskin, 2007, p. 110-111; 132)

Tools for Reconnecting

After about 30 minutes, try to find a way to communicate with each other about reconnecting and calmly discussing the situation. Sometimes more time apart is needed, so I request a specific time to meet before going to bed. I invite you to try to connect and talk through the situation before you go to sleep for the night.

When you both are able to reconnect, I suggest you determine if you are prepared for a verbal discussion or if a somatic (physical/body) release is needed before you are able to be in your body and present with your partner. As a somatic coach, I love re-centering and grounding the body before engaging the heart and mind. If you or your partner are experiencing a lot of pent-up energy/tension, it may manifest as a desire to go for a run, scream, fidget, or punch a pillow. Luckily, there are a number of helpful exercises around energy release that can be done together in a safe and consensual fashion. Like wild and exuberant dancing? Wrestling each other? Or what about a pillow fight? One of my favorites is to have you both step outside or go for a drive and scream out loud at the top of your lungs. Do not scream *at* each other, but simply scream random vowels or curse words together. The object is not to put your partner down, but to release some energy before you return to the discussion.

At this point you have felt tension in your dialogue, called for a timeout using your pre-loaded signal, taken a minimum of 30 minutes apart to care for yourself, and released pent-up energy in your body to feel more grounded. Let's get to dialoguing. First, I invite you to avoid using violent, aggressive, and passive-aggressive language. This time of conflict resolution is about trying to *understand where your partner is coming from*, not beating him to a pulp using your well-sharpened debating skills. Make a commitment to each other not to use language that is cruel or condemning.

Agree not to make any threats of breaking commitments, intentionally harming your partner, leaving your partner, or asking your partner to leave. If you find that either or both of you are unable to uphold these commitments, then use your pre-loaded signal and take another time-out until you are both re-centered and ready to dialogue. It may be helpful for you to journal during this time to sort through your emotions and express them on paper.

....

"This time of conflict resolution is about trying to understand where your partner is coming from, not beating him to a pulp using your well-sharpened debating skills."

....

Alternatively, what if you *cannot* get physical space from each other? I discovered that with practice it is possible to call a timeout from whatever topic is triggering us and go about our lives. For example, perhaps you notice conflict arising between you and your partner, and you realize it is dinner time. Try using your signal for a timeout and go to dinner together with the agreement that neither of you will bring up the triggering subject. Whatever it is or however difficult it is to hold back your words on the subject, you choose to wait and be patient. Talk about the weather, talk about your day at work, talk about your favorite childhood adventure – but do not return to the trigger topic. The fight in you will want to slide in a comment or condescending jab during this timeout.

One exercise that you can do instead of fighting is to both pause and share three things you are grateful for about your partner and your relationship. Gratitude is a powerful tool for healing wounds and can quiet the resentful voices in our heads. Another helpful tip is to remember that you have time set aside in the near future to circle back to this particular topic of conflict. Once you have both eaten and taken at least 30 minutes to recenter, check in with your partner to see if she is ready to use a dialoguing tool. It sounds really hard to do (and it can be!), but with practice it does get easier over time.

....

"Gratitude is a powerful tool for healing wounds and can quiet the resentful voices in our heads."

....

Dialoguing Tools

Through my work with clients and personal studies, I developed a healthy collection of tools and resources for handling conflict, expressing our needs, and developing a deeper understanding of our partners.

My current top-three recommendations include:

- "Aftermath of a Fight or Regrettable Incident" (Gottman & Gottman, 2013) tool from the Gottman Institute. You can get hands-on guided practice if you attend their "Art and Science of Love" workshop.
- "IMAGO Dialogue" by Dr. Harville Hendrix. A detailed explanation of the tool can be found in his book *Getting the Love You Want: A Guide for Couples* (2008).
- *Nonviolent Communication* (NVC) by Marshall Rosenberg (2003). You can read this book, find free videos online, and even attend meetup groups to learn and practice the tool.

I invite you to check them all out and practice the tools together, deciding which are most helpful for your relationship. Don't worry if they feel awkward to use at first – it is often awkward to learn a new skill and flex a new muscle. It takes most clients an average of eight times practicing each one before they feel comfortable using them and can comfortably reap the long-term benefits from the tool. It may be clunky at first, but walking through the dialogue tools together and having a clear, new process for both of you to struggle through at the same time can greatly reduce the amount of drama and conflict that occurs in your relationship.

....

"It may be clunky at first, but walking through the dialogue tools together and having a clear, new process for both of you to struggle through at the same time can greatly reduce the amount of drama and conflict that occurs in your relationship."

....

As you and your partner practice these new ways of handling conflict, I invite you both to keep a somatic awareness. Are you speaking with a calm voice? Are you sitting eye to eye with your partner, or are you standing over her? Status carries a lot of weight in conflict resolution, and we are often unaware of what we project. For example, with one couple that I worked with, Amit is 6'5", and Swetha is 5'9". No matter how hard she tries, Swetha cannot be physically bigger than Amit. Thus, even if he is doing nothing other than standing there, she feels like David facing Goliath. Her natural reaction to threat was to "fight," whereas his was to "flee." So imagine them entering into conflict without being armed, and instead using resolution tools. It's a pretty comical scene where this poor gentle giant tries to escape and she is charging at him full-force, ready to take him down.

It did not take them long to figure out that they needed a better way of fighting. One simple yet profound move that Amit now uses is to physically sit down on the ground when conflict arises between Swetha and him. How could she attack such a small, harmless being? Instead, she found that her natural reaction is to share floorspace and bring her energy lower to discuss whatever is coming up for them. Try it! Next time you are entering an argument, have the taller person sit down on a chair or on the floor, and observe if you have a different reaction to each other.

I also invite you to touch your partner as you move through one of the conflict-resolution dialogue tools that I mentioned. You may not feel like cuddling, but if you are able to hold hands, or even let your shoe rest against his leg, the physical connection can help.

Consider what direction you are looking. Are you both looking forward? Are you looking at each other? Most masculine-energy people handle conflict looking forward. A lot of vulnerability comes out when they are watching a sports

.e. They look forward at the game while talking sideways about what's going on in their life without making eye contact. That's when connection and a lot of growth happens. In contrast, feminine-energy people will often want to get vulnerable eye-to-eye, like sharing deep conversation over a cup of tea. So what happens if you go on a drive where the masculine-energy person is driving and the feminine-energy person is sitting in the passenger seat looking at the masculine-energy person? Through intentionally learning new communication, you begin to change your way of being in ways you might not have been conscious of in the past to create the relationship you desire. I often resolve conflict best while riding in a car, looking forward together, with my hand resting on his shoulder while he drives. Road trips can be a really wonderful time of reconnection and sorting through baggage together.

....

"Through intentionally learning new communication tools, you begin to change your way of being in ways you might not have been conscious of in the past to create the relationship you desire."

....

Fights and conflict will occur in just about any relationship, especially if they are given time and depth. Finding healthy ways to navigate them together and agreeing ahead of time on what kinds of tools you're going to use is incredibly helpful and increases the likelihood that you, your partner, and your relationship will grow together over time.

Take-Away Summary

Conflict is natural in most relationships and will arise at some point throughout your partnership. How you engage with conflict or run from it can be telling of how your relationship will progress. Most people did not grow up with healthy models of how to handle conflict when it arises. I invite you and your partner to create a shared approach for how you can both navigate conflict in a healthy, collaborative manner. This will increase the likelihood that you, your partner, and your relationship will grow together over time.

Here are some helpful tips for how to navigate conflict together:

- Call a timeout when tension begins to rise.
- Create a pre-loaded signal to initiate the timeout.
- Take a minimum of 30 minutes apart to cool down (or at least 30 minutes apart from the triggering topic).
- Practice self-care during your cool-down period.
- Set a time to reconnect and discuss the situation.
- Release pent-up energy in a safe, consensual manner.
- Use an agreed upon *and* pre-practiced dialogue tool.
- Maintain somatic (physical/body) awareness throughout the dialogue.

Invitations (Homework)

❑ 5.1 Handling Conflict
Self-Reflection

❑ **Intention:** To increase your awareness and understanding of how you feel/think/process/hear/understand conflict and what influenced this way of being from your past

∙∙∙

❑ **Implementation:** How was conflict navigation modeled for you as a child? Did your parents/caregivers fight? Scream? Avoid it altogether? A combination? What about for your partner? How did this modeling impact you, and what approach do you each use now? What seems to work, and what makes things worse for you both when conflict arises?

∙∙∙

❑ **Instruction:** Pause, reflect, and journal for 30 minutes. Don't worry about grammar or editing. Allow whatever thoughts there are to flow onto the paper. Try not to stop writing until at least 30 minutes are up. What moments of clarity, direction, depth, and pattern exposure come up for you? Share your take-aways with your partner.

∙∙∙

❏ 5.2 Pre-Loaded Timeout Signal
Exercise

❏ **Intention:** To turn on your creative side and co-create a "secret code" for you and your partner to use as a key communication tool in your relationship

....

❏ **Implementation:** Create a pre-loaded signal with your partner. Remember that it should be easy to do in public and outside of your usual verbiage or body movements to call attention quickly without confusion. What does it mean? Which fears does it help assuage, and which values does it support?

....

❏ **Instruction:** Set aside 10-15 minutes to create a signal that works for both of you. Do this one time, then practice implementing your signal at least once per day for the next two weeks. You may do a "practice drill" or actually use the signal and then follow the appropriate steps outlined in the chapter when conflict arises.

....

❑   **5.3 Applying Dialogue Tools**
     Exercise

❑   **Intention:** To apply the cognitive learning tool
     in daily life and make it more accessible in your
     relationship

     ....

❑   **Implementation:** Choose a dialogue tool from the
     ones mentioned in this chapter. Read through the
     instructions or watch an online video for clarity.
     Practice it together at least 3 times in low-stress
     situations. When ready, move on to a higher-stress
     situation. Using a new conflict-resolution tool is
     often a bit awkward the first dozen times you use
     it – remember, you are learning something new! It
     is okay to be students together. If a tool does not
     resonate with you after a few practices, try one of
     the others listed.

     ....

❑   **Instruction:** Set aside 20 minutes for easier topics
     and at least 60 minutes for more challenging topics
     to complete the exercise. Have one person kick off
     the tool, then switch roles, giving time and space
     for both people to use their voice and hear their
     partner. Debrief on what went well and what would
     work better in the future.

     ....

6 Avoiding Unwanted Surprises

What Constitutes a Surprise?

Adam:

Next up, we have one of my favorite agreements: "avoid surprises," which we used to call "no surprises." (We discovered this is impossible.) So what is a surprise? Let's talk about great surprises first. My partner is phenomenal at surprising me in ways that make me feel loved and cherished. The surprise trip to Hawaii on my 35th birthday was a great surprise. I also appreciate surprises like coming home from a hard day and finding brownies on the counter with a nice note, getting a raise, or hearing that my child learned a new word. There are really great surprises in this world, and it's important to notice and appreciate them.

There are also what I call "unwanted surprises." We discovered throughout reflecting on our relationship and making agreements together that most of the really hard stuff was precipitated by unwanted surprises. For example: "I know it wasn't on my calendar, but I've decided I'm going to go to Portland for two weeks, starting tomorrow morning. I realize that maybe you had some other thoughts on how we would spend some time together, but this is what I want to do." Surprise! Or: "Your mother-in-law is coming tomorrow to stay with us for an indefinite amount of time." Surprise! Unwanted surprises can also be small, day-to-day events that can have a significant impact: "I forgot to warn you that I have a huge work deliverable due this week, and I need to miss our dinner plans to work late."

....

"We discovered throughout reflecting on our relationship and making agreements together that most of the really hard stuff was precipitated by unwanted surprises."

....

Why do unwanted surprises hurt? An unwanted surprise feels uncomfortable because we don't have time to process the new information, ask questions about it, or sit with it; it's happening now. Situations that we would have digested and accepted with conversation and time are painful when they show up as unwanted surprises. We can avoid most unwanted surprises through effective and welltimed communication and writing into our Relationship Agreements how and when this communication should happen.

....

"We can avoid most unwanted surprises through effective and well-timed communication and writing into our Relationship Agreements how and when this communication should happen."

....

Timing Is Everything

Eri:

Time is an important resource, with implicit scarcity, in relationships; unwanted surprises regarding time and commitments can be very hurtful. Committing to weekly calendar sync-ups (I recommend Google Calendar) is a phenomenal way of drastically reducing unwanted surprises. During a weekly calendar sync-up, look at your calendars together, schedule time together, look at items that have shown up on your calendar throughout the week, and go over what the next couple weeks may look like.

Discussing trips, plans, and other commitments in advance can help avoid unwanted surprises around time and scheduling. Here are what experts Dossie Easton and Janet Hardy have to say about the importance of predictability and avoiding unwanted surprises:

What Other Experts Are Saying

"Our experience is that we need some sort of predictability... Most people can handle a nervous-making situation much better if they know when it is going to happen and when it is going to be over. You can plan to do something supportive with a friend, go to a movie, visit Mom, whatever – and tell yourself that you only have to handle things for this chunk of time...

Most people have a hard time dealing with surprises, which can feel like land mines [sic] exploding... If you feel that planning takes too much of the spontaneity out of your life, then think about declaring one night or one weekend a month to be open season;... an agreement to be unpredictable at some specified time is, after all, predictable." (Easton & Hardy, 2009, p. 155-156)

Adam:

Knowing what is emotionally charged and particularly important for you and your partner is helpful in avoiding unwanted surprises. Talk about where your values lie; understand your and your partner's values and emotional attachments. Communication around what we value and where our emotional attachments are can be a great tool to avoid surprises. Here's an example of emotion-based values and how they affect my relationship to holidays and their celebrations, which has been very useful for me to share with my partner. Thanksgiving is really important to me. I value great food, being surrounded by friends, and quality connection time with my loved ones.

Because I communicate this value to her, it won't come as a surprise when that's where I put my energy during the holiday. On the other end of the spectrum is Valentine's Day. I don't have any emotional attachment to Valentine's Day. If I don't communicate my lack of emotional attachment and she goes out of her way to buy me roses and chocolate, there is an unwanted surprise and disappointment that could have been avoided by talking about our values and attachments. In a similar way, people often have strong emotions attached to finances. How can you avoid surprises around finances? If you're getting married, looking to get married, or are entering some sort of domestic partnership, we suggest you make agreements around how you will each handle finances or combine finances. Making these agreements can help you avoid a conversation like, "Hey, I just bought a car with our savings. I didn't know you were saving up for a house!" Thinking ahead, where do your values lie? What are your triggers? What consensus needs to be reached ahead of time to avoid surprises for everyone involved in your Relationship Agreements?

....

"What consensus needs to be reached ahead of time to avoid surprises for everyone involved in your Relationship Agreements?"

....

A simple practice I have found to be particularly useful is that when I'm about to schedule something, I am thinking about making something happen in my life, or something I am excited about shows up for me, I ask myself two questions: "How can I make this not a surprise? What can I do besides putting it on my calendar to help this be understood more clearly, sooner?" Just as the Relationship Agreements are evolving and impermanent, so is your reaction and your partner's reaction to surprises. The better you know someone and the more time you've been together, the less likely it is you will unintentionally surprise or be surprised.

....

"When I'm about to schedule something, I am thinking about making something happen in my life, or something I am excited about shows up for me, I ask myself: 'How can I make this not a surprise?'"

....

Here's an example: In the past, you wanted a month to plan a vacation. Now, you know that you and your partner both like certain things, and you know your partner's going to plan a vacation that is going to be fantastic or spontaneous in a way that you appreciate with a 24-hour notice.

Your request: "I would really like to plan a vacation a month in advance" can change to: "I'd like to plan three days in advance," or: "I'd like to plan while on the flight." Recognizing the shift when your needs for safety and structure have changed, reassessing your needs and values, and communicating these changes to your partner will mean these agreements can shift and change. Regular check-ins help to reduce unwanted surprises and enable you to support each other better.

Be Realistic

Eri:

It is unreasonable to expect that there will never be unwanted surprises in your relationship. The reason I recommend changing the wording in your Relationship Agreements from "no surprises" to "avoid surprises" is because it is nearly impossible for surprises not to show up. We are not robots; we are humans. Surprises will occur. I invite you to brainstorm hypothetical situations that could arise in your relationship and talk through how you might handle them together. Having some idea of what you *might* need to face together gives you creative solutions for similar surprise realities that will occur.

There will be little landmines along the way. What matters is how you prepare for the explosion and handle the aftermath together, reducing the risk of harm as much as possible. Avoiding surprises is going through the minefield that is your relationship and digging out the mines that are quite obviously placed in front of your path. You won't be able to clear all of them. You won't be able to get the ones buried deeply or the hidden ones. But the ones that are on the surface, that you can clear out ahead of time with a little bit of extra practice and care – each one you find and address lessens the chances of unwanted explosions.

....

"There will be little landmines along the way. What matters is how you prepare for the explosion and handle the aftermath together, reducing the risk of harm as much as possible."

....

What happens when we *do* set off one of these unwanted surprise landmines? This is where the conflict navigation dialogue tools from the previous chapter come in handy. Together, create a space where both you and your partner can feel honored and safe. Talk through what happened and what could have been done to prevent it from being a surprise. Are there any agreements you can put into place to reduce future risk? Talking through the situation as soon as you are able helps quiet the monsters in our heads and lessen the blow of future explosions.

Take-Away Summary

Surprises are a part of life – we can't eliminate them, but we can reduce the occurrences of unwanted surprises and thus reduce conflict and stress. A few ways to help make this happen can be to have regularly scheduled times for syncing up on life and schedules; openly sharing your values and emotional attachments; being realistic; and practicing regular check-ins. Remember that there will still be landmines along the way. Be prepared to talk through them and create agreements to prevent future similar explosions.

Invitations (Homework)

❑ ## 6.1 Preparing to Avoid Surprises
Self-Reflection

❑ **Intention:** To increase your awareness of how you and your partner understand and process your triggers around feeling surprised

....

❑ **Implementation:** Where do your values lie? For example, perhaps time management is a big value for you, and a lack of shared value in this area might lead to unwanted surprises. What are your triggers around being surprised? What agreements need to be made ahead of time to avoid surprises for everyone involved?

....

❑ **Instruction:** Pause, reflect, and journal for 30 minutes. Don't worry about grammar or editing. Allow whatever thoughts there are to flow onto the paper. Try not to stop writing until at least 30 minutes are up. What moments of clarity, direction, depth, and pattern exposure came up for you? Share your take-aways with your partner.

....

❑ 6.2 Looking Out for Potential Landmines
Self-Reflection

❑ **Intention:** To bring awareness to the past and create an opening for dialogue around being proactive in avoiding landmine explosions within your relationship

....

❑ **Implementation:** Brainstorm hypothetical "landmine" situations that could arise (or already have!) in your relationship and talk through how you might handle them together in the future. What "landmines" have you encountered in past relationships that you can prevent from exploding in this one? If you could do it all over again in this relationship, what would you change? How could you implement those changes now?

....

❑ **Instruction:** Pause, reflect, and journal for 20-30 minutes. Don't worry about grammar or editing. Allow whatever thoughts there are to flow onto the paper. Try not to stop writing until at least 20 minutes are up. I encourage you to repeat this journal question more than once if needed. Share your take-aways with your partner.

....

7 Check-Ins

Channeling Our Emotions

When it comes to relationships, our emotions can play a crucial part in how the story unfolds. Most of us were raised with extreme ways of handling our emotions: to either repress them or inappropriately express them. As Karla McLaren so beautifully explains, there is another way – one that fortifies the ideal relationship we are co-creating.

What Other Experts Are Saying

"Both repression and expression can be helpful to us in certain situations, but they cannot between them address every emotional situation we encounter. Take repression, for instance. When you are infuriated at a baby, repressing the fury is a good idea – it's never right to express fury toward a baby. But once we've repressed the fury and made the baby safe, we need to be able to address the fury in private, or it will rear its head once again, perhaps with more energy the next time. Because here's the situation: emotions are always true – they always tell the truth about how you're actually feeling – but they may not always be *right* or appropriate in each situation. Therefore, we have to learn how to understand, interpret, and work with them, and we must find the middle path between repression and improper expression. We must learn to honor and attend to our emotions in a deeper, more mature, and more evolved way. We must learn not to work *against* the emotions with repression or *for* the emotions with incompetent expression. We must learn to work *with* our emotions.

There is a middle ground in the emotional landscape; there is a way to work with emotions in a respectful and honorable way. I call the process *channeling* the emotions, by which I don't mean to suggest some metaphysical of calling for disembodied spirits. I'm referring to the actual meaning of the word 'channel,' which is to direct or convey something along a chosen pathway in a conscientious manner. If we can learn to properly channel our emotions, we can begin to work with them in vibrant and ingenious ways. We can interpret the messages our emotions carry and make use of the instincts our emotions contain.

The hand-off we do with emotional expression – that hand-off to the outer world – doesn't bestow any skills upon us. Likewise, the hand-off we do with repression, when we shove our emotions back into the inner world, makes us even less skilled. Neither approach works because neither one accepts emotions are useful as messengers that help us learn and evolve. When we stop handing off our emotions, and instead learn to channel them honorably, we can take our emotions into our own hands. We can listen to them, feel them consciously, and express them in ways that will bolster our self-image and our relationships, rather than tearing them down." (McLaren, 2010, p. 32-33)

Learning to express our emotions in mature, healthy ways can strengthen our communication and reduce conflict. Having a developed sense of awareness around your emotional landscape and how to channel your emotions will not only help prevent large conflicts, but will also help you identify the need for a check-in with your partner.

Let's Pause and Clarify

Check-ins are simply time set aside to discuss a topic or event that might feel a bit more emotionally charged. Reasons for a check-in can be wide ranging and diverse. When we go about our relationships with the idea that everything's going to be just fine, hunky-dory, and no manner of upset will emerge, we set ourselves up for disappointment. The truth is each day contains moments where a pause or more clarification would be useful in our relationships. Check-ins are particularly handy when a situation occurs with our partner that feels disagreeable. Perhaps our brain or heart asks us for more information, but our voice doesn't get onboard. When this happens, we create stories and look for reasons to pacify and justify our reaction. If we had just asked in the first place, there'd be less worry or fear and fewer "monster stories" being created. Emotionally charged circumstances will almost always exacerbate a situation, when all we need is additional context to soothe the anxiety around jaggedness and difficulty.

> *"When we go about our relationships with the idea that everything's going to be just fine, hunky-dory, and no manner of upset will emerge, we set ourselves up for disappointment."*

Here is an example of a check-in:

"Hi, Love, I had some concerns about something that happened a moment ago (or earlier today, or yesterday, or last week), and I'm looking for some clarification around it. I'd love some more ease in my understanding of what has happened (or what will happen, or what is happening right now). Would you be willing to set some time aside either right now or in the near future, so that we can chat about this? I think it will take about 5 minutes to discuss."

Keeping check-ins hemmed in and succinct will allow for a feeling of security to coalesce. Solid time boxes ensure that it won't feel like an all-day procedure. The likelihood of a positive outcome for your check-in will go up significantly. If the topic requires more time, use the check-in to block off more time in that moment, or for later in the day/week when you can both meet and discuss it using one of the conflict-navigation tools mentioned in Chapter 5.

....

"Keeping check-ins hemmed in and succinct will allow for a feeling of security to coalesce."

....

Mitigating Fear

A concern I've heard from numerous clients is something like this: "OK, my partner requested a check-in. Now I'm going to spend the rest of the time worrying what it might be about until we can make the check-in happen."

In order to mitigate that fear, I find it helpful for the person who is requesting the check-in to state the topic in just a few words or short phrases. Concise, contextual, compassionate, and comprehensible. Perhaps it's around time management. Maybe it's about the fight you had earlier. Or maybe it's around our upcoming mother-in-law's visit. Sharing the check-in topic beforehand can keep old stories and monsters in your partner's head from wreaking havoc on something that is not actually of concern at this time.

....

"Sharing the check-in topic beforehand can keep old stories and monsters in your partner's head from wreaking havoc on something that is not actually of concern at this time."

....

Conversely, I encourage you not to launch into the full topic of the check-in at the time you're proposing it. This can be both unnecessarily time wasting and potentially triggering. Brevity is your friend, here. Think title of a book chapter, not a trailer that gives away the entire movie. Setting time aside for your check-in for later that night or the following day can help with feelings of urgency and anxiety around not being "ready." As busy as some of our lives are, inserting a potentially disrupting conversation into the middle of a day already in progress might not be prudent.

This is a tool that requires practice! I find that, with most couples, there is at least one person who wants to launch into the depths of the discussion when a check-in is requested. This is not the point. This tool creates space for you to talk about it later, at a more appropriate time, while still noting that it's worth exploring later. Be patient. Try it out – it just may help make life a little easier.

Self-Care Prior to Check-In Time

Be prepared for your check-in with your partner by checking in with yourself and using some of the tools I referenced in Chapter 6 on Conflict Resolution. Have you eaten recently? Are you well hydrated? Have you gotten enough rest? If this is potentially a triggering topic, try taking a 20-minute nap beforehand. Is there anything else frustrating or exhausting that happened earlier in the day? This might be useful to have awareness around before beginning your check-in. Is there something you can do to re-center and be present for your partner as he brings up a topic that is challenging? The objective of the check-in is for discovery, resolution, and clarity. If you find that you're going into it looking for conflict, try to find out why that might be. Conflict may arise, regardless. However, the adversarial position is often times an old pattern that is no longer helpful and will prolong the disconnect between you and your beloved.

••

"The objective of the check-in is for discovery, resolution, and clarity."

••

Another example might be a missed opportunity or appointment between you both. Perhaps there wasn't any communication around it other than the acknowledgement of its existence. Resentment might start to build, and a voice might start to whisper: "What if my partner is going to be missing future appointments? What if this is a streak of lackadaisicalness or lack of follow-through that is going to continue?" A check-in might be useful to say, "Hey, I noticed that you missed our appointment earlier (or the thing we said we were going to do together). I'd love to know why that happened and how we can avoid this in the future. Can we talk about that in 20 to 30 minutes?" It can really be something as simple as that. Setting time aside to bring clarity (or resolution!) to the perceived trespass or the giant question mark can feel like a big relief.

Take-Away Summary

A check-in is an opportunity to set aside time to discuss a topic or event that might feel a little heavier than the usual fare. This tool can help you pause and clarify situations throughout your day – especially when one arises that feels disagreeable with your partner. Asking about the circumstance early on can lessen worry or fear and quiet the "monster stories" being created in our minds.

A few helpful hints on how to use check-ins include keeping them succinct; stating the topic using concise, contextual, compassionate, and comprehensible language (not launching into the full topic); and being prepared by first checking in with yourself before using the tool with your partner. The objective of the check-in is for discovery, resolution, and clarity.

Invitations (Homework)

❏ 7.1 Checking In
Exercise

❏ **Intention:** To apply the cognitive learning tool in daily life and make it more accessible in your relationship

....

❏ **Implementation:** Practice asking for a check-in with your partner. Begin using less triggering topics and work up to more difficult ones. Practice it together at least 3 times in low-stress situations. When ready, move on to a higher-stress situation. Using your voice to break old patterns can often feel awkward at first. Remember, you are learning something new! It is okay to be students together.

....

❏ **Instruction:** Set aside 5 minutes for easier topics and at least 10 minutes for more challenging topics to complete the exercise. Have one person at a time request a checkin, then switch roles, giving time and space for both people to use their voice and hear their partner. Debrief on what went well and what would work better in the future. With practice, most check-ins of any topic require around 30 seconds to 2 minutes of your time.

....

❑ 7.2 Checking In on Our Check-In
Self-Reflection

❑ **Intention:** To help you pause and reflect on your current way of being; this reflection will bring awareness to how you react to this check-in tool and help you connect with yourself and your partner more authentically

....

❑ **Implementation:** When practicing the check-in, what came up for me? How did my body respond to hearing a request where I simply acknowledged the need to talk through it at a later time instead of immediately trying to fight through or resolve it? What happened between the time a check-in was requested and the time we actually set aside to discuss the issue? What might prevent me from successfully using the check-in tool? Why? What can I do to set myself up for success in the future?

....

❑ **Instruction:** Pause, reflect, and journal for 10-15 minutes at the end of each day. Don't worry about grammar or editing. Allow whatever thoughts there are to flow onto the paper. Try not to stop writing until at least 10 minutes are up. I encourage you to repeat this journal question daily for one week. At the end of the week, reread your journal and look for moments of clarity, direction, depth, and pattern exposure.

....

8 Creating YOUR Relationship Agreement

Where to Begin: Personal Work

One of the first questions I often hear when I talk about the process of creating Relationship Agreements is: "How do I get started?" After helping numerous clients create and revise their Relationship Agreements multiple times over the course of many years, I suggest that personal work followed by a staycation is the best place to begin creating this powerful tool together. This chapter will focus on these two elements. However, if you are unable to take a staycation for whatever reason, I encourage you to use the sample staycation schedule in Chapter 9 and hold "mini-sessions" together each week as time and resources allow over the course of a month. My "Final Note" to you at the end of the book contains additional ways to design your Relationship Agreements while being supported in the way that best fits you and your relationship.

Personal Work

What do I mean by "personal work"? Recall in Chapter 1 when I touched on Personal Agreements – creating a document that reflects who YOU are and what you value in life and relationships. This is a central part of taking the time to be alone and think through what matters to you before meeting with your significant other to create a Relationship Agreement. If you do not have the time/space/desire to create a Personal Agreement at this moment, I encourage you to complete the Self-Reflection Invitation at the end of this chapter to help prepare you for beginning your Relationship Agreement dialogue. Personal work allows you to stay present and "hold on to yourself," as David Schnarch (1997) puts it, as you design your ideal relationship with your partner.

What Other Experts Are Saying

"'Hold onto yourself' is a simple idea with many meanings. Self-mastery and self-control involve learning about yourself, confronting yourself and shifting to self-validated intimacy, and taking care of yourself (self-soothing). Learning to hold onto yourself nudges your personal development and your marriage forward, and fundamentally changes how you and your partner interact. Holding onto yourself is a shorthand way of talking about differentiation... Holding onto yourself – maintaining a relationship with yourself – is not easy. However, the benefits to you and your marriage are incalculable... Your marriage is a complex system geared around self-mastery. Emotionally committed relationships respond better when each partner controls, confronts, soothes, and mobilizes himself/herself – and that's exactly what dynamics in your relationship will push you to do." (Schnarch, 1997, p. 323-325)

The Staycation

I suggest you and your beloved commit at least two consecutive days on your calendars every four to six months for this Relationship Agreements staycation. Get away from your everyday environment. This is an incredibly important element. It changes the way you naturally respond to the patterns (healthy and unhealthy!) you and your partner have built over time and creates more space for curiosity and new ways of being. Perhaps you can do a house-swap with friends or use a travel website to find a place to relax and reconnect. Having it planned ahead of time and seeing it on the calendar is an important part of preparing and getting excited for this time. I invite you to view the Relationship Agreements staycation akin to one of your favorite holidays and count down the days until you and your beloved will share wonderful, intentional exploration time together. In Chapter 9, I will give detailed schedule suggestions for how to invest in your time together.

....

"I invite you to view the Relationship Agreements staycation akin to one of your favorite holidays and count down the days until you and your beloved will share wonderful, intentional exploration time together."

....

Before you head out on this adventure, make sure you pack for the event. Bring your favorite foods, apparel, and hobby gear. I've now worked with several couples in different countries who love to connect through partner dance. I encourage them to be intentional about brining music they both love to dance to and setting aside time for connecting through dance on both days of their escape. In a similar vein, it is important to set aside time for intimate connection to explore each other's bodies and celebrate your love. The Relationship Agreements staycation is *not* all-business-all-the-time; it is intentional time together, deepening the relationship and sharing vulnerability.

....

"The Relationship Agreements staycation is not all-business-all-the-time; it is intentional time together, deepening the relationship and sharing vulnerability."

....

During these two days, there is a very good chance one or both of you will be bringing up possible trespasses done since the last time you talked about your Relationship Agreements.

Or, if you are creating your Relationship Agreement for the first time, you might feel trepidation about what your partner may request during this process. Being prepared to create a safe and loving environment (e.g., nourishing food, tools for connection, comfortable lodging) will help ease stress when you need to take a break due to emotions running high. Give it some space, do something different for yourself or your relationships, re-nourish your body and your heart, and return to the crucial conversation re-centered.

I encourage you to approach this time co-creating your Relationship Agreements together with care and compassion; make it sacred. Our culture today is one that focuses on staying busy, and we have all but lost the value of ceremony, save for really big events like weddings. Having a regular ceremony or ritual around building your relationship together can be very powerful and can strengthen the bond between you. This might include talking about the upcoming staycation or upcoming date with hope, excitement, and joy around growing together and celebrating where you've been, including the times when you have fallen on your faces. Many juicy discussions are rooted in learning together from past mistakes. If you enter this space with a heart of love and forgiveness, it can have many positive impacts on your relationship – in addition to the process of creating agreements together.

. . . .

"I encourage you to approach this time of co-creating your Relationship Agreements together with care and compassion, and make it sacred. Our culture today is one that focuses on staying busy, and we have all but lost the value of ceremony. Having a regular ceremony or ritual around building your relationship together can be very powerful and can strengthen the bond between you."

. . . .

Adam:

This time of creating, re-creating, modifying, and checking up on your Relationship Agreements is intended as a time for joy, discovery, curiosity, and questioning. This is not about strife or punitive measures. You and your beloved are choosing to check the foundation of your relationship, make sure it's strong, bolster the weakened points, and grow ever further upward together.

....

"This time of creating, re-creating, modifying, and checking up on your Relationship Agreements is intended as a time for joy, discovery, bewilderment, and questioning."

....

Self-Development, Self-Awareness, and Self-Care

Some of the most successful relationships I have encountered are those where the individuals invest a large amount of energy and intention toward continuing to explore and develop themselves. They have a keen sense of their inner self and know how to care for themselves emotionally, physically, mentally, and spiritually. They are able to nurture their relationship, their partner, and themselves – creating and sustaining a holistic system of support.

While on your staycation, I invite you to set aside some time to be alone and do self-care. If it is already built into your weekend, it will be easier to move into time by yourselves. Stay flexible in your schedule and request alone time when either of you feel like time is needed to regenerate your energy and refocus. When you pause to be still, it becomes easier to hear whatever is going on inside of you. Your inner voice will reveal incongruity and help you make authentic Relationship Agreements with your partner based on where you are along your personal journey.

• •

"Your inner voice will reveal incongruity and help you make authentic Relationship Agreements with your partner based on where you are along your personal journey."

• •

Self-care looks different for each person. Try experimenting with different tools to discover how your body and soul respond best to being cared for and nourished. Get a massage. Go for a long walk in nature. Lie by a body of water, listening to classical music. Read a good book. Eat fresh produce from a farmers market. Journal. Meditate. For ideas on timing and tools for re-centering when you are feeling triggered, please see the section in Chapter 5, "SelfCare during Cool-Down Period."

The more self-awareness and vulnerability you can share with your partner, the greater the likelihood your beloved will reciprocate the same awareness and vulnerability. Plugging into yourself and your relationship during this time together will make a huge difference in how this time – and ceremony – will unfold.

• •

"The more self-awareness and vulnerability you can share with your partner, the greater the likelihood your beloved will reciprocate the same awareness and vulnerability."

• •

Unplugging

Because our society is so driven to be plugged into technology all the time, I encourage you to unplug from your gadgets during this time together. It is far too easy to let the weekend slip away consumed by e-mails, text messages, and YouTube videos. If you are able, turn off your cell phones, go off the grid, and make a commitment not to be working on your careers/social life. Focus on each other and your connection together. If you have children, this is a good time to leave them with other caregivers and make sure you have some sacred space for the two of you as lovers and partners. It is important to focus on the relationship you share together and not have to constantly switch gears to the demands of technology, children, and work. This is a time for you to work solely on your relationship.

Help – I am Freaking Out or Feeling Resistant!

You and/or your partner may be feeling nervous about or resistant to going through this process and creating a Relationship Agreement. Your feelings are valid! I am inviting you to try something that is out of most people's comfort zones. Writing down mutual agreements in our romantic lives flies in the face of what our media and culture tells us to do. If maintaining healthy, invested relationships built on trust, communication, and integrity were easy, then we would see far fewer relationships ending in fiery explosions and resentment. What you are choosing to do together by intentionally designing your ideal relationship is bold, courageous, and off the beaten path. It makes a lot of sense that you might hold a lot of strong emotions around it. I invite you to recognize your feelings, and create enough space for you to let go of old stories and habits that may no longer serve you. Keep this open curiosity long enough to create your Relationship Agreements together. This is a well-tested tool that continues to have major positive impacts on couples around the globe. Perhaps it is worth experiencing for yourself.

. . . .

"What you are choosing to do by intentionally designing your ideal relationship together is bold, courageous, and off the beaten path."

. . . .

Zen Reminders

- Creating your Relationship Agreement is a *choice* to invest in your relationship.
- Your Relationship Agreements are a living document. You can change it as needed to expand and contract – reflecting your lives and the relationship in the moment.
- Relationship Agreements are not legally binding, and the spirit of the agreement is to grow and love deeply together.
- Relationship Agreements are built on honesty, trust, and integrity by consenting adults.
- Relationship Agreements have been used by many people around the globe and have been shown to reduce conflict, strengthen communication, and increase intimacy. Perhaps it's time to invest in your own Relationship Agreements and experience them for yourself!

Take-Away Summary

Preparing for co-creating your Relationship Agreement takes time and intention. Do your homework beforehand, and plan your stay-cation in advance. There are some wonderful exercises for these steps in the following "Invitations" section in the next few pages. The purpose of this time together is to design, modify, and check up on your relationship while sharing joy, curiosity, and discovery.

Here are a few highlights for this time: be intentional about having a heart of love and forgiveness; set aside some time to be alone and practice self-care; unplug from your gadgets and turn your focus inward to yourself and to each other during this time together.

If maintaining healthy, invested relationships built on trust, communication, and integrity were easy, then we would see far fewer relationships ending in fiery explosions and resentment. Be gentle with yourselves as you maneuver through this process of designing your ideal relationship together. Remember that this is a living document and is not legally binding. Know that you are not alone in this journey – this tool has been used by many people around the globe and has been shown to reduce conflict, strengthen communication, and increase intimacy. Ready to experience it for yourself?

What you are choosing to do together by intentionally designing your ideal relationship is bold, courageous, and off the beaten path. It is worth celebrating!

Invitations (Homework)

❑ ## 8.1 Preparing for Your Staycation
Exercise

❑ **Intention:** To stimulate a holistic mindset of how you approach preparing for your staycation; to strengthen intention for a weekend of deep connection and growth

....

❑ **Implementation:**
Personal Preparation Questions
  ❑ Personal Work – have you created a Personal Agreement for yourself? Have you completed the invitations in this book?
  ❑ What kind of self-care tools/resources might you find most helpful during your staycation? Make sure to pack what is needed.

Staycation Preparation Questions
  ❑ Which dates can you block off on your calendars (Friday night through Sunday evening)?
  ❑ Where will you stay?
  ❑ What foods do you need to purchase/prepare ahead of time?
  ❑ What do you need to pack?
  ❑ What miscellaneous things do you need to pack, including a journal, hiking shoes, a swimsuit, surprises for your partner (perhaps a new sexy toy to experiment with together), a speaker to play music from, a yoga mat, etc.?
  ❑ How will you get there?

❑ Do you need to hire childcare ahead of time? Can your parents/friends take the children?

❑ Do you need a pet/house sitter?

❑ Do you need to let colleagues know you will be off-grid all weekend?

....

❑ **Instruction:** Set aside whatever time is necessary for you in your current lifestyle to read through and complete these questions. Read through them at least a week prior to your staycation. Add any additional questions/task items of your own that would be helpful. Be sure to partner with your beloved to share in the responsibility, and co-create the experience together.

....

❑   **8.2 Contemplating Your
Preparation Experience**
Self-Reflection

❑ **Intention:** To increase your awareness and
understanding of how you feel/think/process/
hear/understand your world

....

❑ **Implementation:** As you move through the questions
in Exercise 8.1, notice how you are feeling. Is there
anything you need to check in with your partner about
prior to the staycation? What is going smoothly?
What is more challenging than you expected? What
are you surprised by? Is there anything you need to
request help with? Is there anything that needs to
change?

....

❑ **Instruction:** Pause, reflect, and journal for 5-10
minutes at least 3 times prior to leaving for your
staycation. Don't worry about grammar or editing.
Allow whatever thoughts there are to flow onto
the paper. Try not to stop writing until at least 5
minutes are up. Share any highlights with your
partner prior to your trip, and hear how the process
is going for her.

....

9

Samples to Get You Started

In this chapter, I will provide a few suggestions for how to use your staycation time and what you might consider exploring in your own Relationship Agreements. I have seen everything from 4 bullet points total to 41 pages of physical expressions of Relationship Agreements. How you decide to use your Relationship Agreements staycation time and the format you choose to reflect your "Fred" is as unique as your relationship. My hope is that these samples will get your creative juices flowing while providing enough structure to help you navigate these waters together. Have fun. Get messy. Make it YOURS.

* *

"How you decide to use your Relationship Agreements staycation time and the format you choose to reflect your 'Fred' is as unique as your relationship."

* *

First-Time Sample Staycation Schedule
Day 1 (Friday Night)

Time	Activity	Notes
7:00-8:30pm	Dinner Together	Bring or buy something we both love!
8:30-9:30pm	Unwind & Connect	• Share a drink by the fireplace, go for a walk along the beach, etc. • 3 things I am grateful for about my partner • Hopes and Fears for creating a Relationship • Agreement together
9:30-11:30pm	Physical Connection	Take time to slowly reconnect intimately. Perhaps we take a hot bath together or explore a fun fantasy we have been talking about sharing.
11:45pm	Sleep	Snuggle and get some rest. We have a big weekend ahead of us!

Day 2 (Saturday)

Time	Activity	Notes
9:00-10:30am	Sleep in and start the day together	Morning intimacy followed by the "5 Breaths" exercise*
10:30-11:30am	Brunch	Consider making your favorite food together while dancing to great music.
11:30am-2:30pm	Relationship Agreements Dialogue Block 1	• Values Exercise* • Share the top 3 topics for each of you or use the "Lean Coffee" Exercise* • Prioritize order for discussion of all 6 topics** (or fewer if some are the same) • Topic 1
2:30-3:30pm	Self-Care Break	Take some alone time to journal, go for a walk, take a nap, etc.
3:30-4:00pm	Quick Lunch	Consider sharing sandwiches in the sun.

*See "Invitations" at end of chapter.
**See "Sample Relationship Agreement Topics"
below the sample schedule.

4:00-7:00pm	Relationship Agreements Dialogue Block 2	• Topic 2 • Topic 3 • Topic 4
7:00-8:30pm	Dinner Together	Bring or buy something you both love!
8:30-9:30pm	Connect & Have FUN	Play a game, tell silly stories from our childhood, etc.
9:30-11:30pm	Physical Connection	Take some time to slowly reconnect intimately. Perhaps play Betty Martin's "3 Minute Game"* listed in the references section at the end of the book.
11:45pm	Sleep	Wow! We did SO much today for US!

See "Invitations" at end of chapter.

Day 3 (Sunday)

Time	Activity	Notes
8:00-9:00am	Sleep in and start the day together	Morning intimacy followed by the "5 Breaths" exercise*
9:00-10:00am	Breakfast	What would we both really love to eat for the staycation breakfast?
10:00am-2:00pm	Relationship Agreements Dialogue Block 3	• Check in on how this experience is going for each of us • 3 things I am grateful for about my partner • Topic 5 • Topic 6 • Extra wiggle room baked in for further discussion (adding/changing our Relationship Agreements doc, creating a conflict resolution plan for triggering subjects, etc.)
2:00-3:00pm	Lunch	How can we have fun together over lunch? Food fight? Picnic? Unexpected cuisine? Feeding each other food while taking turns being blindfolded?

See "Invitations" at end of chapter.

3:00-4:00pm	Self-Care Break	Take some alone time to journal, meditate, go for a walk, take a nap, etc.
4:00-7:00pm	Relationship Agreements Dialogue Wrap-Up	• What we want to discuss next time • Schedule next staycation • How did it go? Play "The Perfection Game"* • Share gratitude with each other for the time, love, and intention we invested in our relationship.
7:00-7:30pm	Cuddle and Connect	Just chill and enjoy being together. No more seriousness. Laughter welcomed!
7:30pm	Closing	End our time together with a long hug and the "5 Breaths" exercise* before returning to our usual lives (kids, careers, social commitments, etc.).

*See "Invitations" at end of chapter.

Sample Relationship Agreement Topics

These sample topics are taken from living documents and are ever changing, just like the people involved. This is list not exhaustive! My clients are continually thinking of new topics that are unique to them. Perhaps some of these can be broken down into even more detailed subtopics for your relationship. Use what works for your relationship and let go of the rest. I suggest completing Invitation 9.2 for insights into your personal values to help determine which topics you will explore together and what priority they are given.

· ·

"Use what works for your relationship and let go of the rest."

· ·

- **History:** how our Relationship Agreement came into fruition and how it evolved over time
- **Overview:** who we both are as a couple; a clear definition of what our relationship means (what does *marriage/ co-parent/partner* mean to YOU?); a statement of our responsibility for self; a commitment to growth and harmony; and a definition of our roles in this relationship
- **Wellness:** how we care for each other with compassion; how we care for ourselves; how we grow not just in mind and body, but in spirit, too
- **Intimacy:** how we connect through physical, emotional, spiritual, and sexual time together; how we explore fantasy; who initiates intimacy; how often we engage in intimate behavior; our sexual and romantic levels of exclusivity and monogamy; how we communicate and share vulnerability in this space; how we make requests; how we accept or decline invitations; how we get our needs met
- **Autonomy:** what is the appropriate balance for us as individuals and as a couple?
- **Communication:** how we trust and honor each other; "Inquire Within"; use of check-ins; avoiding surprises; our "Love Languages" (Chapman, 2015); connection time; commitment to calendaring/scheduling; how often and via what means we communicate; rules of engagement; replacing veto power
- **Outward Facing:** family; co-parenting; vacations; finances; travel
- **Relationship Resources:** great tools and resources we find along our journey to help us grow together

- **Future Topics to Explore:** an ongoing list of subjects we might want to discuss and add into our Relationship Agreements

Hopefully these section titles hold a few gems for what you might like to explore with your partner and include in your Relationship Agreements. Relationships take work, but they can also be a lot of fun. They grow over time, and become beautiful experiences to share with someone you love. My hope is that you find this tool to be as useful as I have, and that it will give you the freedom to stretch your wings together over time.

Take-Away Summary

There are countless ways to design and format your own Relationship Agreement. How you decide to use your time during the staycation and reflect your "Fred" is as unique as your relationship. Test out the tips and tools suggested. In the end, use what works for your relationship and let go of the rest. Remember to have fun, get messy, and make it YOURS.

Invitations (Homework)

In this chapter, I am suggesting many helpful tools that I often lead my clients through during workshops and that will move you smoothly through the staycation together. Many of these tools come from my days working in information technology, especially the world of Agile Programming. I invite you to try them all and see which ones resonate with you both as you move through your staycation together.

❏   ## 9.1 "5 Breaths"
Exericse

❏   **Intention:** To be reminded that taking deep breaths to begin each new day of your staycation together will help set the tone for the day and help you be intentional about your time together

....

❏   **Implementation:**
1.   Stand with your feet hips-width apart or sit in the lotus position.
2.   Have your beloved stand or sit in front of you, and hold hands.
3.   Close your eyes.
4.   With the first inhale & exhale, practice your smiling muscles.
5.   With the second inhale & exhale, fill yourself with gratitude.
6.   With the third inhale & exhale, forgive others.
7.   With the fourth inhale & exhale, forgive yourself.
8.   With the fifth inhale & exhale, set your intention for the day.

9. When you are both finished, I invite you to end
    with a smile and a kiss.

....

❑ **Instruction:** Take 5 full, deep breaths like this at
the beginning of each new day. You may repeat
with your partner as often as desired. If some steps
require more time than a single breath, do not rush
the exercise. Simply go at your own pace and signal
your partner with a hand-squeeze when you are
finished.

....

❏ 9.2 "Personal Core Values" (Mind Tools, 2016) Exercise

❏ **Intention:** To explore your personal values in depth and share your findings with your partner to gain a better sense of how each of you places weight and value on choices and agreements you make; to help give direction as you design your ideal relationship together; to help prioritize what to focus on in the first iteration of your Relationship Agreement

....

❏ **Implementation:** Complete the "Personal Values" exercise from Mind Tools:

- Step 1: Identify the times when you were happiest.
- Step 2: Identify the times when you were most proud.
- Step 3: Identify the times when you were most fulfilled and satisfied.
- Step 4: Determine your top values, based on your experiences of happiness, pride, and fulfillment.
- Step 5: Prioritize your top values.
  (Mind Tools, 2016)

....

❑ **Instruction:** Set aside 60 minutes to go through the questions and subquestions (explained in depth on the website https://www.mindtools.com/pages/article/newTED_85.htm). Seriously, go to this website link – the questions listed above will be explained clearly and with great depth for ease of exercise completion. Discuss your answers with your partner and look for ways in which your values might influence your Relationship Agreement. How might you order your Relationship Agreement topics of discussion during your staycation based on this exercise?

❑   9.3 Values and Boundaries
Self-Reflection

❑ **Intention:** To increase your awareness and understanding of how you feel/think/process/hear/ understand your needs, values, and boundaries; to help prioritize what to focus on in the first iteration of your Relationship Agreement

....

❑ **Implementation:** What topics are important to be included in a Relationship Agreement (e.g., finances, chores, sexual connection, personal growth, family, time management, communication, spiritual growth, health and wellness, conflict resolution)? What boundaries are valuable in your relationship? (Hint: if you are unsure what boundaries you want to keep, reflect on moments when your partner – or past partners – did something that triggered an angry response in you. Anger is usually a sign that we fear our boundary being threatened.) What new question(s) arise from what you observed in this self-reflection?

....

❑ **Instruction:** Pause, reflect, and journal for 30 minutes. Don't worry about grammar or editing. Allow whatever thoughts there are to flow onto the paper. Try not to stop writing until at least 20 minutes are up. Share any highlights with your partner.

....

❑ ### 9.4 "Lean Coffee" (LeanCoffee.org, 2013)
Exercise

"Lean Coffee" is not actually about coffee at all (though you are welcome to enjoy a cup while you use this tool). It is a way of structuring a dialogue or a meeting without setting an agenda (a tool I learned from my years in the world of information technology). As you sit down to do this exercise, you can create the topics together and immediately begin talking. This tool relies only on you both showing up and wanting to learn and create together.

··

❑ **Intention:** To provide a fun, structured tool to help move through topics of discussion in a time-bound and creative manner

··

❑ **Implementation:**
1. Gather a pad of Post-it notes and a pen for each person.
2. On the table in front of you, create 3 columns: "To Discuss," "Discussing," and "Discussed."
3. Designate a timekeeper.
4. Set a timer for 5 minutes. During this time, each of you individually will create 1 topic per Post-it note that you would like to potentially discuss for your Relationship Agreement. Add these under the "To Discuss" column.
5. Once the time is up (or you have finished creating your topics list), each person will introduce their topic Post-its with 1-2 sentences.

6. Each of you now gets 3 votes on the topics you think are of highest priority to cover during the staycation. You may vote for your own topics. You may also vote multiple times for the same topic.
7. Tally the votes and stack-rank the topics to create a discussion order.
8. Place the topic with the most votes under the column "Discussing."
9. Set a timer for 21 minutes.* During this time, you may both take turns discussing this topic.
10. After the timer goes off, take a quick vote. On the count of "3," put your thumb up for "Yes, let's keep talking about this," thumb pointing sideways for "I am neutral on whether we should continue or move on to the next subject," or thumb down for "I feel this topic is complete. Let's move on."
11. If you choose "yes" after 21 minutes* are up, reset the timer for 15 minutes*, and then continue taking turns discussing this topic. If you are both "neutral" or indicate "no," move the topic Post-it to the "Discussed" column and choose the next topic to discuss.
12. After the 15 minutes* are up, take another quick vote. If either or both of you indicates "yes," set the timer for an additional 6 minutes* and continue discussing this topic.
13. Once the final timer (6 minutes*) goes off, the topic is closed for this round. You may revisit it later, but for the time being, move the topic Post-it to "Discussed" and choose the next topic.
14. Each topic should take no more than 45 minutes* to discuss.

*For the quicker, leaner version of the tool, divide the total time listed (also marked with an *) for each activity by 3. (E.g., each topic should take no more than 15 minutes to discuss.) Since you have almost a full hour set aside to discuss each juicy topic, this tool will help guide you along and keep you on track.*

....

❑ **Instruction:** Play this game at the start of your Relationship Agreement Block 1 to help create the structure for your discussion blocks, and then refer back to it as you move through each topic at the scheduled time.

....

❏   9.5 "The Perfection Game" (Linders, 2014)
Exercise

❏ **Intention:** To use a fun and unique way of delivering and receiving feedback together; to find actionable steps you can take together in the future

....

❏ **Implementation:**
1. Rate the experience: On a scale of 1-10 (with 1 being "I would never want to take another staycation/creating a Relationship Agreement with you is not for me"; and 10 being "That was the best relationship-building experience of my life!"), how did the staycation and designing your own Relationship Agreement together go?
2. State what you liked. What went well, and what made it so great?
3. Suggest what to do to make it perfect. What can be improved when we take our next staycation and revisit our Relationship Agreement together?

....

❏ **Instruction:** Play this game at the end of your Relationship Agreement staycation during the wrap-up to collect feedback and decide what you would like to do differently next time to make it closer to perfect for both of you.

....

10 We Did It! Now What?!

Congratulations! You have completed your Relationship Agreements! This is a time for celebration and honoring all of the hard work, love, and intention you invested into your relationship. As I mentioned earlier in the book, your Relationship Agreements will not have a specific length or look. This is YOUR creation and is unique to you. Maybe it is 4 bullet points long, or maybe it is 20 pages with graphics. Now how do you make sure the growth you experienced does not get lost and forgotten in the midst of life's usual chaos?

Make It Accessible

I invite you to print a copy and hang it where you will both be able to see it on a regular basis. Refrigerator doors and bathroom mirrors are often ideal places. I also encourage you to save a copy on your smartphone for easy access anytime and anywhere, should you need a reminder or a check-in about your current agreements.

Look for ways to keep your Relationship Agreements fresh in your minds and hearts. Perhaps choose an agreement to read together each week over Sunday dinner or create an anagram to help you memorize your agreements (if they are not too long). One of my client couples creates a keyword or short phrase every two weeks to remind themselves about a section they want to focus on from within their Relationship Agreements. They write it on Post-it notes in visible places around their home, car, and work. This keeps their different agreements fresh and allows them both to be more conscious about specific elements they want to highlight.

....

"Look for ways to keep your Relationship Agreements fresh in your minds and hearts."

....

Revisiting and Revising Your Relationship Agreements

Finding the right rhythm for you to review your Relationship Agreements will be important. The most successful stories I have heard are when people plan their staycation once a quarter or once bi-annually. I suggest starting with whichever of these resonates most with both of your current schedules and then modifying as necessary.

Sample Veteran Staycation Schedule

For those who have already created their Relationship Agreements, I suggest a similar schedule as in Chapter 9, but with the following changes:

Relationship Agreements Dialogue Block 1	Retrospective: Re-read everything we wrote together. What went well since the last time we reviewed our Relationship Agreements? What did not go so well? What could we have done differently to have greater success? What do we want to change in the current text?

Relationship Agreements Dialogue Block 2	What do we want to add/remove? Are there big topics we have not yet addressed? Prioritize them and start working through each one.
Relationship Agreements Dialogue Block 3	Continue adding more topics/revisions. Leave space for difficult discussions and use our conflict navigation tools.

Broken Agreements

As mentioned in Chapter 6, we, as humans, are fallible. It is inevitable that one of you will mess up and break an agreement at some point in time, whether intentionally or unintentionally. The goal is to find ways to stay connected and talk through the pain. These situations are rarely easy to navigate, and there are incredibly powerful tools available to help guide the conversation and heal the wounds. If this is something you are experiencing, I encourage you to begin reading *Forgive for Love* by Dr. Frederic Luskin (2007) and using the Gottman Institute's "Aftermath of a Fight or Regrettable Incident" tool (Gottman & Gottman, 2013) – both referenced in Chapter 5.

· ·

"It is inevitable that one of you will mess up and break an agreement at some point in time, whether intentionally or unintentionally. The goal is to find ways to stay connected and talk through the pain."

· ·

It is important to note that if you are in an abusive relationship where you or your partner use a pattern of abusive and coercive behaviors to maintain control and power over the other, more work needs to be done before forgiveness can occur. Please seek professional help to break the cycle and create healthy new patterns together.

What Other Experts Are Saying

"Forgiveness is an inside job: it has a direct bearing on your ability to cope with your relationship and helps you come to peace so that you can make the best decisions... Forgiveness reminds you that it is not just what your partner does, or does not do, that causes you pain. Much of your suffering comes from having wanted your partner to do something different from what he or she actually did... Forgiveness contains the understanding that another person's action, no matter how awful, does not compel you to be endlessly miserable, angry, or emotionally distraught... Research shows that by healing the past, forgiveness can provide a more peaceful present... Having a forgiving nature is a powerful thing and can profoundly improve our relationships." (Luskin, 2007, p. 15-21; 57-59)

You Are Not Alone

People across the world have been creating Relationship Agreements, learning through their failures, and celebrating their successes. You are not alone. This book serves as a starting point for you to create a deeper, more intimate, and more connected relationship that changes and grows with you over time. If you are feeling stuck or desire more depth with this type of relationship work, I invite you to use the resources at your fingertips. Check out the References and Suggested Further Reading section at the end of this book, reach out to local organizations that help foster healthy relationships, build a network of support around your relationship, ask around about who else has created their own Relationship Agreements, and work with a professional coach or therapist. In addition, I invite you to read my "Final Note" to you at the end of this book for more personalized ways in which I can support you and the success of your relationship.

Take-Away Summary

You've completed your first Relationship Agreement! It is time to celebrate and honor all of the hard work, love, and intention you have invested into your relationship. (Seriously – go out and celebrate over a drink/dinner/adventure date. Woot!) Here are your next steps: make your Relationship Agreement accessible, schedule your next staycation *now*, be proactive by preparing for when a trespass does happen, explore your resources, and know how you can get support.

Invitations (Homework)

❑   ## 10.1 Fresh & Refreshing
Exercise

❑   **Intention:** To keep the momentum from your work together; to make an action plan for holding your Relationship Agreement in your heart and mind

....

❑   **Implementation:** Create an action plan together for how you will make your Relationship Agreement accessible in your daily lives. Consider saving it to your smartphones, securing a printed copy to the refrigerator door or bathroom mirror. Perhaps leave a copy in the glovebox of your vehicle. Once you have your plan in place, go do it! Use this time and momentum to complete it and have it out there for you. Finally, use your calendars and schedule your next staycation. I suggest 3-4 months out from now.

....

❑   **Instruction:** Set aside 30-45 minutes to create *and complete* your action plan and calendaring.

....

❑ 10.2 Read *Forgive for Love* by Dr. Frederic Luskin (2007)
Exercise

❑ **Intention:** To open your mind and heart to a potentially new concept and give you tools proactively

....

❑ **Implementation:** Read and complete the exercises from Luskin's book: *Forgive for Love* (2007). Take note of any key concepts, new ideas, challenging views, and discuss them with your partner.

....

❑ **Instruction:** Set aside at least 20 minutes per day to read and work through this book. Debrief with your partner once you have both completed each chapter.

....

❑ **10.3 Roses and Thorns Retrospective**
Self-Reflection

❑ **Intention:** To pause and reflect on how the entire process went of taking a staycation and co-creating your Relationship Agreement to bring awareness to what may need to change and what to incorporate again in the future

....

❑ **Implementation:** What were the "roses" (the beautiful, magical parts that stand out and that you may want to repeat)? What were the "thorns" (things that were unpleasant or challenging)? Try to identify at least 1 rose and 1 thorn from each category: pre-planning, staycation preparation (logistics), preparing yourself, Day 1, Day 2, Day 3, and returning to the "real world."

....

❑ **Instruction:** Pause, reflect, and journal for 15-20 minutes about the experience of taking a staycation and co-creating your Relationship Agreement. After you have each completed your individual journal reflections, share your thoughts with each other for 30 minutes. Decide how you will handle the "thorns" for next time, and create more openings for "roses" together.

....

11 Application for Ethical Non-Monogamy

As I mentioned in the "How to Use This Book" section, this book is written for *you*. I have applied these concepts and tools to relationship structures of all types with people from diverse cultures all around the globe. Whatever identifying labels you connect with (straight, gay, lesbian, transexual, queer, monogamous, polyamorous, swinger, open, etc.) and whatever cultural and religious values you hold, this book contains tools to navigate partnership challenges and design your ideal relationship. That being said, the first 10 chapters of this book are written for everyone to read and apply. In this chapter I will speak directly to people who choose a less traditional relationship structure: ethical non-monogamy.

What is *ethical non-monogamy*, and why is there a chapter dedicated to it? In my private coaching practice, I often work with people who choose ethical non-monogamy as their preferred relationship model. This blanket term means that they choose to be sexually, romantically, maritally, and/or emotionally involved with multiple consenting adults while being transparent about their lifestyle and setting clear boundaries and agreements together. They may choose it right from the start of their relationship, or they may decide to open their marriage a decade later. Many of these people identify as being "open" in their relationships and use labels such as *polyamorous, swinger, poly fidelity, partnered non-monogamy,* or *solo poly.*

Another form of non-monogamy that can be done ethically and is common in mainstream culture is what most people refer to as *single and dating around*. It is not uncommon for people to go on dates with multiple people in a week/month when they are single and looking for their soulmate(s). How much you choose to disclose about dating others and the types of health risks you are taking/sharing with your dates is what puts you into what I would consider the "ethical" category or not. You probably know someone who has cheated on a partner or has been cheated on by someone they trusted to be faithful. This is unethical behavior. Ethical non-monogamy is designing your own relationship boundaries and agreements together. Breaking these guidelines would be considered unethical.

There are many resources available to learn more about these lifestyle choices. If you are in search of more information on the subject (or any subject discussed in this book), please contact me and check out the resources listed in the back of this book. Today extensive information on the subject is easily accessible to us via online blogs and websites, books common in local libraries, educational workshops hosted at your local adult stores, private social media lifestyle groups, meetups, and "sex-positive" resource centers found in most major cities in the USA. *Sex-positive* refers to an attitude that promotes safer, consensual sexual exploration for adults. The resources I list in this book are just a few of my favorites for people beginning to explore more options of alternative relationship structures.

I do not believe there is any "right" relationship structure – just what is right for you in this moment. People who choose less mainstream paths must create their own boundaries, agreements, ceremonies, and rituals. For those who choose monogamy, I encourage you to learn about tools and techniques used in open relationship models. Many of the lessons learned from ethical non-monogamy can benefit monogamous relationships, too. For example, several of my clients that I work with come into my coaching practice having already learned tips for how to handle jealousy; how to communicate better; and how to be open, honest, and authentic with partner(s) at all times from the polyamorous (i.e., "many loves") culture.

··

"People who choose less mainstream paths must create their own boundaries, agreements, ceremonies, and rituals. Many of the lessons learned from ethical non-monogamy can benefit monogamous relationships, too."

··

In this chapter, I will provide a few examples of how some of the previous sections could be applied to an ethically non-monogamous model. This chapter is meant to complement previous chapters and provide a window into how others can and are using Relationship Agreements in their partnership(s), no matter which structure they choose. But first, let's see what Taormino has to say about creating a Relationship Agreement (which she refers to as a *contract*) and how it can apply to ethical non-monogamy.

What Other Experts Are Saying

"As part of the negotiation process for a BDSM [Bondage and Discipline (BD), Dominance and Submission (DS), Sadism and Masochism (SM)] scene or a relationship, some kinky people write and sign a contract to outline their limits and what they've agreed to. Even if you are uninterested in BDSM, I recommend you borrow this practice from the world of BDSM. A relationship contract can be a useful tool in negotiating your nonmonogamy. This contract is not a legal document, but rather a written agreement in which you clearly articulate your needs, wants, limits, rules, expectations, goals, and commitments.

Writing a contract is a helpful exercise for really nailing down what you want; it may get you thinking about things you never considered. One of the benefits of a contract is that it makes the terms of your relationship real; it can strengthen your bond, since you commit to what you put on paper and to each other. It can help prevent miscommunication, and it can serve as a reference point for resolving it, especially when people don't remember exactly what was said about a particular issue ('I thought you said –' 'I thought you meant–'.) Trust me, it's much better to ask for clarification when you're negotiating the contract rather than when you're in a hotel room about to have sex with someone! You can return to the contract periodically to check in with each other and revise your agreement.

Here are some elements you can incorporate into a relationship contract:

- A statement about the nature of your relationship and your commitment to one another
- A statement about your personal values and philosophies
- What you hope to achieve through nonmonogamy
- The rules or guidelines for: who, what, when, where, other partners, safe sex
- Other pertinent limits and boundaries
- Schedule of time and date commitments
- The process for starting a relationship with a new partner
- The process for airing grievances
- Agreement about being 'out' to other people
- Explanation of how to amend the agreement

While a contract can clarify your agreement and commitment to one another, it is not a guarantee of anything. A contract will not make your nonmonogamous relationship perfect. A contract cannot prevent miscommunication, misunderstanding, or irresponsible or hurtful behavior. It should not be used to justify behavior after the fact: 'Our contract didn't say anything about strippers in other countries.' The contract is a tool for communication and clarification, not a weapon to be wielded against someone later. No matter how thorough you are, a situation will probably arise that is not covered by the contract; remember that it's not only about what is on paper in black and white; it's about the *spirit* of the contract. While a contract can bring clarity, it is not meant to set anything in stone. Your relationship, limits, and boundaries will change – your desires and sexuality may change subtly or dramatically – and your agreements should change with them." (Taormino, 2008, p. 148-150)

Taormino provides excellent insight into the possible uses of Relationship Agreements within the sex-positive world. As mentioned in Chapter 2, she reiterates the importance of keeping the *spirit* of the agreement as you design and navigate your relationship together. I encourage you to reflect on which elements came to mind for you when you read her suggestions for what to incorporate into your ethical non-monogamous Relationship Agreement.

How a Relationship Agreement Will Transform Your Relationship (Chapter 1)

In this chapter, I invited you to create your own "User Manual." For those exploring ethical non-monogamy, Cunning Minx of PolyWeekly.com shares her "User Manual" on her website. I invite you to use it as a starting point as you create your own. Here are the main section titles and a few examples of what she includes:

What Other Experts Are Saying

"Part A: Family Background/History

- Again, I didn't have a close family, and I tend to be kind of awed by people who have good relationships with their relatives. I think that is why I like the idea of poly-amory – my family of birth isn't going to suddenly be all lovey dovey and supportive, so wouldn't it be cool if I could have a family of choice that was, just so I could have that experience? That would be nifty.

Part B: How to Turn Me On Emotionally

- Ask your partner to reach out to me. I love being welcomed into an existing relationship; it can start to feel like family to me. If you're in an existing relationship, ask your partner to chat with me, reach out to and welcome me. I've had far too many metamours who ignore or tolerate me turn out to be hiding insecurities and resentment and causing considerable damage, both to me and to their existing relationships. If she can muster up a nice, warm welcome or at least a friendly chat, these fears will quickly be allayed. If she can't, I'll quickly bow out.

Sexually: Flirting

- I have a lot of interests, not just sex, poly and kink. If you love to cook, I would love someone to cook an elaborate dinner with. If you are into interior design/ home renovation, I'd love someone to brainstorm and carry out home improvement projects with. If you dance, I'd love someone to hone my dance skills with. If you travel, I'd love someone to go on vanilla trips with sightseeing in Europe, relaxing on the beach in Mexico, exploring Tibet. Love wine? I love going to wine bars and trying a flight with complementary cheeses.

Sexually: Sex

- People often ask me what I'm into sexually. And in truth, the answer is, 'It depends.' There are a few activities I know I enjoy, to be sure. I've discovered, though, that it's often not the activity; it's the dynamic between the people and their respective levels of enthusiasm for and skill at the activity that matters. If you do something really well or have some special skill or kink, just let me know. Even if it's not my favorite thing now, it might be with you. And my favorite thing now might not be all that great with you. Let's just see what we're into together, shall we? That being said...

Turn-Ons (With Consent):

- Grab the hair at the roots at the back of my neck. This is a trigger for me.

Turn-Offs:

- Not getting tested. Not being willing to wear protection and not getting tested regularly for STIs are hard limits for me. And not just AIDS, full blood tests for everything." (Cunning Minx, 2011)

One of the things I enjoy about Cunning Minx's "User Manual" is her ability to be direct and authentic, while still connecting with the reader. I invite you to be courageous and include as many key points that you are comfortable sharing with potential/new partners. Don't worry; there will still be many discoveries remaining about each other, your families of origin, and your individual quirks as time goes on.

"Inquire Within" (Chapter 3)

"Inquire Within" can be an incredibly useful tool in open relationships. As mentioned in the chapter, there have traditionally been two main polarized paths for sharing sensitive information: "Don't Ask Don't Tell" (DADT), or the "Firehose Method." In DADT, partners commit to not sharing any information about dates, love interests, or Internet romances with their beloved(s) in an effort to reduce drama and hurt. I do not advocate this choice, but I have seen it work effectively for a *very* small number of people. The Firehose Method takes the other extreme: partners share EVERYTHING about their dates and interests, including emotional, physical, and spiritual connection information in full detail, whether their partner wants to hear it all or not. I suggest trying out "Inquire Within" as a middle option for communicating. This allows for receivers of the information to determine what they feel is important to hear. Perhaps this night they want to know about the emotional connection you shared with a new love, but they do not care about the physical interaction play by play.

An example might be something akin to talking about a new interest or someone you have been flirting with. Perhaps you've already started to explore something with this new person, or in the event that something already happened – you may be returning home from a date. Your partner may be curious about how this is shaping up, what activities occurred, and what the future holds.

Using "Inquire Within," a gradual discussion is safely unfurled, where sensitive subjects can be arrived upon intently without feeling as though too much or not enough information is being shared. This also enables requesting information regarding the goings-on of partners (past or present) to feel comfortable. Here's an example of an "Inquire Within" check-in that might take place after returning home from a date:

Kris: "Hi, hon!"

Tristan: "Hey!"

Kris: "How'd your night go?"

Tristan: "The night went really well."

Kris: "Oh, you just got back from your date, right?"

Tristan: "Yes! Yes, I did."

Kris: "How did it go?"

Tristan: "First, Sheila and I went to dinner and shared some fantastic conversation. We ate dessert, we danced, and then we went back to her place."

Kris: "Sounds like you had a good time!"

Tristan: "We did."

Kris: "You said that you went back to her place. Does that mean you both had a chance to share some intimacy?"

Tristan: "We did. Is there something specific you'd like to hear about, or are you looking for more of an overall?"

Kris: "Tonight I am not feeling in the mood to hear any juicy details; I would appreciate more of a chapter stop. If you could let me know how far you went physicaly, that would help me feel less anxious."

Tristan: "Sure! So, we had some nice snuggle and kissing time; we got undressed and explored some touch and manual play, too. We stopped the night's activities at just using our hands, though."

Kris: "That sounds like a solid place to begin your exploration, and it also sounds like you really liked being with Sheila. Do you think you'll continue seeing her in the future?"

Tristan: "Yeah, I think we might have a few more dates. I'm not sure as to the longevity of it, but I'm really enjoying the physical connection right now, and I want to respect what we've already talked about with regard to sexual safety. So, I'm choosing to keep it at manual play for right now."

Kris: "Sounds good. If you decide to advance any further and there is any risk of STIs or anything else you think I should be aware of, I know you'll check with me before you proceed."

Tristan: "I absolutely will. Thanks for asking for what you wanted. I really appreciate it."

Kris: "I'm glad you had a great date."

Tristan: "Thanks, I did."

Please note that "Inquire Within" does *not* mean that the person sharing the information has the right to omit pertinent information if the leading person does not ask the right question. Prior to using this tool, make an agreement that the person sharing will quickly volunteer any information that may be crucial to the health and safety of the receiver (e.g., STI risk of transmission *prior* to engaging physically). This will reduce harm and lower the risk of unwanted surprises.

Replacing Veto Power (Chapter 4)

Veto Power is a tool often used in open relationships. A common example might be something akin to: "I don't want you to date this person or spend intimate time with this person because I just don't like her/she's too pretty/I dislike the way she relates to me. You are not allowed to date that person anymore." In most examples I have observed, veto power ultimately fractures the relationship – maybe not right away, but the ramifications are profound over time.

As I mentioned in Chapter 4, I invite you to try having those difficult conversations about how you are feeling, your fears, and your requests. For relationships that are ethically non-monogamous, the question of veto usually arises when one partner is tempted to veto a potential new partner. It is important to remember that if your partner is dating a new person, she is most likely under the biological influence of being "twitterpated" and may not be able to see the situation from an objective standpoint. You can compassionately share your concerns about the potential new partner and any perceived risk to the health of your relationship.

Once your partner has heard you, allow her time to reflect on your perspective and then make her own decisions. If each of you continues to operate from a place of love, intention, authenticity, and respect for your relationship, there are great chances that she will navigate this complex situation well, making her own decisions as she goes and checking in with you along the way.

Avoiding Unwanted Surprises (Chapter 6)

A surprise that might come up in an ethical nonmonogamous relationship is something like: "Hey, I just met someone. I think they're amazing, and we're going on a date tonight," even though your partner may have requested a three-day notice before you go on a date with a new person. Situations like this one where a request (especially if it is an agreement!) is not being honored can be poisonous to your relationship and trust in each other. Instead, try to find creative ways to navigate the interaction in order to maintain the rhythm and stability in your relationship.

It may be helpful for you and your partner to clarify what you agree to communicate about new potential partners and when to share this information with your beloved. This might include your intentions with the new person, your level of interest or connection, and any large points of discussion to consider in a timely fashion (whatever that might mean for you both). It is helpful to recognize that sharing this information can often feel uncomfortable and difficult to convey. Expressing gratitude for your partner's courage in demonstrating integrity, compassion, vulnerability, and forthrightness can help build trust and confidence in your connection. For a fantastic example of how you can craft your own conversation around difficult personal topics, I invite you to check out "Reid's Safer Sex Elevator Speech" (2011) listed in the reference section of the book.

....

"Expressing gratitude for your partner's courage in demonstrating integrity, compassion, vulnerability, and forthrightness can help build trust and confidence in your connection."

....

If you are someone who is concerned about how "serious" a new partner might be for your lover, I have a tool you can test out. It is not perfect, but it can help you understand the depth of initial perceived connection. When your partner meets a new love interest, ask him to categorize the level of connection as either a "Puddle," "Pond," or "Pacific." You can define these terms in whatever way best fits your dating style. For example, a "Puddle" may be someone he finds attractive, but simply desires a fling with. A "Pond" may be someone he sees staying in his life for 3-6 months and enjoying each other's company, romance, or physical connection. A "Pacific" may be someone he envisions being partnered with for a lifetime. I have found this information to be helpful for the person hearing about the new potential relationship (i.e., the *metamour*) because it provides a sense of what type of connection he currently shares with this new person, and it tells you how connected he might want to become with this new person. For example, upon hearing that he has a potential "Pacific" in his life, you may decide to reach out and share coffee with this new person sooner rather than later. After all, there is a good chance you both will be connected via your partner for quite some time!

Even if you are experienced with open relationships, there will almost always be new and challenging circumstances to learn from. Creating hypothetical situations and talking through how to handle them together can prevent many unwanted surprises, but not all of them. Here is a real-life example of an unforeseen communication glitch: Juliet met Liam online and introduced him virtually to her fiancé, Todd, before going on a wonderful date with Liam. They stayed within the physical boundaries of the sexual safety agreements she had with Todd. However, she did not communicate to Liam about how she and Todd had agreed to share information with each other. (I talked about information sharing in the "Inquire Within" section.)

The unfortunate, and avoidable, fallout of this was that Liam shared information with Todd while they were chatting online shortly after the date Liam had with Juliet. Liam assumed they had a "Firehose Method" approach to sharing details and informed Todd of details he was not prepared to hear about the date (including sexual interactions). This was not in accordance with the agreements Todd and Juliet had in place. Liam meant no harm and thought it was okay to share since they were in an open relationship. However, this led to Todd being unpleasantly surprised by the information and needing to set very clear boundaries about how, when, and who he wants to communicate with regarding partner interactions.

They didn't foresee some of the complications of this situation. Juliet didn't consider asking her new lover not to share information with Todd. It happened, and they learned how to avoid similar unwanted surprises in the future. They now know to talk to their partners about communicating how the date went or how the relationship is going with their significant other – not leaving it entirely up to them, but still leaving some room for creativity if they want to connect or go out for coffee.

Check-Ins (Chapter 7)

A great time to use a check-in for an open relationship might be when you're having some sort of emotional reaction to your metamour (your partner's other partner). For example, maybe you're dealing with some feelings of jealousy as your partner is going on a date tonight. Maybe you don't have a date scheduled and are feeling grumpy that she is going out and you are not. Request a check-in to express these emotions and ask to validate them. Feeling heard can help quiet the inner voices of panic, jealousy, or fear of abandonment. You're not asking your partner to change her behavior – simply to empathize and hold space for you while you are in a tough spot. Maybe she can even check in later on to see how you are feeling. Or perhaps she might be willing to send an extra text message before she goes to bed – reaffirming that love and connection while muting the wails of abandonment.

Creating YOUR Relationship Agreement (Chapter 8)

Here are a few examples of topics I have seen people in open relationships use in their Relationship Agreements. I invite everyone, whether you are monogamous or ethically non-monogamous, to communicate about these important topics:

- Dating & Communication
- Language Definitions (e.g., *partner* vs. *lover* vs. *play partner* vs. *wife*)
- Boundaries (emotional, sexual)
- Sexual Safety (what to test for, how often, how to disclose results in a respectful manner, sharing physical connection with people with positive STI results, staying up to date on medical findings around STIs – and not social stigma/rumor/lack of education)
- Sexual Expression Exploration including Consensual Kink/BDSM (What are your fantasies? Mine? What might we be open to exploring together and under what circumstances? What about with others?)

The world of ethical non-monogamy has many great examples of Relationship Agreements since this culture is very comfortable redefining what a relationship looks like for them. Whether you choose a monogamous or ethically non-monogamous relationship model, I encourage people to seek out examples that others have created and learn from their experiences.

Take-Away Summary

I encourage you to choose a relationship structure that is right for you and the place you are at in life. Whatever that decision (and it may change over time!), I invite you to remain open to the idea that people who make choices different from your own can have nuggets of wisdom for you. The world of ethical non-monogamy holds an incredible number of powerful relationship success tools that can be applied to monogamy. Whichever relationship structure is right for you, I encourage you to seek out stories, tools, and wisdom from people of all backgrounds of experience. The more resources you have, the more you have to pull from to design your ideal relationship.

Invitations (Homework)

For those of you in relationships that are ethically non-monogamous, I invite you to return to each of the exercises mentioned at the end of each chapter in this book. If you did not do so the first time around, complete the invitations from the perspective of being in an open relationship. Use the tips and examples from Chapter 11 to prompt additional thoughts, reflections, and questions. Please share with your partner(s) when relevant.

Conclusion

It is my hope that this guide has inspired you to take the courageous step of designing your ideal relationship by co-creating your very own Relationship Agreements that will grow and change with you over time. This tool has been proven to strengthen communication, reduce conflict, and increase intimacy. I invite you to create your own, and share your experience with those around you who might benefit from a new approach to their relationships. May this be a helpful resource for empowering you to choose your own adventure in relationships, love, and life!

References and Suggested Further Reading

Chapman, G.D. (2015). *The 5 Love Languages: The Secret to Love that Lasts.* Chicago, IL: Northfield Publishing.

Cunning Minx. (2011, April 19). RTFM: The User Manual. *Polyamory Weekly.* Retrieved from http://polyweekly.com/2011/04/rtfm-the-user-manual

Easton, D. & Hardy, J.W. (2009). *The Ethical Slut: A Practical Guide to Polyamory, Open Relationships, & Other Adventures.* Berkeley, CA: Celestial Arts.

Gottman, J.M. & Gottman, J.S. (2013). The Art and Science of Love: A Weekend Workshop for Couples. *The Gottman Institute, Inc.*

Gottman, J.M. & Silver, N. (2000). *The Seven Principles for Making Marriage Work: A Practical Guide from the Country's Foremost Relationship.* New York, NY: Three Rivers Press.

Hendrix, H. (2008). *Getting the Love You Want: A Guide for Couples.* New York, NY: Henry Holt and Company, LLC.

Labriola, K. (2010). *Love in Abundance: A Counselor's Advice on Open Relationships.* Eugene, OR: Greenery Press.

Labriola, K. (2013). *The Jealousy Workbook: Exercises and Insights for Managing Open Relationships.* Eugene, OR: Greenery Press.

Lean Coffee Lives Here. (2013). *LeanCoffee.org.* Retrieved from http://leancoffee.org/cities-with-lean-coffee

Linders, B. (2014, January 14). Getting Feedback with the Perfection Game. *BenLinders.com*. Retrieved from https://www.benlinders.com/2014/getting-feedback-with-the-perfection-game

Luskin, F. (2007). *Forgive for Love: The Missing Ingredient for a Healthy and Lasting Relationship*. New York, NY: HarperCollins Publishers.

Martin, B. (n.d.). 3-Minute Game. *BettyMartin.org*. Retrieved from http://bettymartin.org/category/3-minute-game

Martin, B. (n.d.). The Wheel of Consent. *BettyMartin.org*. Retrieved from http://bettymartin.org/videos

McLaren, K. (2010). *The Language of Emotions: What Your Feelings Are Trying to Tell You*. Boulder, CO: Sounds True, Inc.

Mihalko, Reid. (2011, August 12). Reid's Safer Sex Elevator Speech. *ReidAboutSex*. Retrieved from http://reidabout-sex.com/safersexelevatorspeech

Mind Tools Editorial Team. (2016). What Are Your Values? Deciding What's Most Important in Life. *Mind Tools Ltd*. Retrieved from https://www.mindtools.com/pages/article/newTED_85.htm

Perel, E. (2007). *Mating in Captivity: Unlocking Erotic Intelligence*. New York, NY: HarperCollins Publishers.

Riley, J. (2014). *Trust Issues: Manage the Anxiety, Insecurity, and Jealousy in Your Relationship with 10 Simple Steps*. (4th ed.). Amazon Digital Services, LLC.

Rosenberg, M.B. (2003). *Nonviolent Communication: A Language of Life*. Encinitas, CA: Puddledancer Press.

Ryan, C. & Jethá, C. (2010). *Sex at Dawn: The Prehistoric Origins of Modern Sexuality*. New York, NY: HarperCollins Publishers.

Schnarch, D. (1997). *Passionate Marriage: Keeping Love and Intimacy Alive in Committed Relationships*. New York, NY: W.W. Norton & Company.

Schwartz, J. (2017, January 5). Communication & Sex & Relationships, Oh My! *The Huffington Post*. Retrieved from http://www.huffingtonpost.com/entry/communication-sex-relationships-oh-my_us_586e5b46e4b07888d4813e84

Taormino, T. (2008). *Opening Up: A Guide to Creating and Sustaining Open Relationships*. San Francisco, CA: Cleis Press, Inc.

Veaux, F. & Rickert, E. (2014). *More Than Two: A Practical Guide to Ethical Polyamory*. Portland, OR: Thorntree Press.

Gratitude

- Contributing Author: Adam Kardos – without you this resource would not be as powerful, magical, and experiential-based. I am so honored to share life with you!
- Editor: Michelle Lingo – words cannot describe how amazing you are and how your editing skills took this book to the next level. I am grateful for our professional partnership.
- Transcriber: Emily McGrath – for the amazing speed you have in transcribing, and for the support our families share with one another.
- Formatting Team: AtriTeX Technologies, LTD. – such amazing speed, skill, and professionalism!
- Cover Designer: Ida Fia Sveningsson – you have an amazing eye for design and such patience for your clients! Thank you for all of your creativity and openness to suggestion.
- Photographers: Josh Wisely, Pablo Argon, and Alyssa Chartrand.
- Marketing Manager: Tyler Wagner of Authors Unite – your guidance and insights into navigating the world of publishing are priceless.
- Photographers: Pablo Argon (back cover) www.PArgPhoto.com, Josh Wisely (About the Author image) www.JoshWisely.com, Jeff LaPlante (About the Contributing Author image) www.JeffLaPlante.com.
- Jaymin Patel – my life partner and soulmate, without you this book would not have been birthed when it was calling to come out. Our "Life of AND" together is powerful and transformational. Each day I look forward to partnering with you and designing the next chapter of our story.

- Aavi Kardos – our magical son who went on so many adventures with us while mommy created this book for the world (17 states and 5 countries before you turned 1 year old!).
- "Baby Bean" – who gave me the extra creative energy and a timeline to make sure that I delivered this book before I delivered you into the world.
- Jeremy and Karissa Lightsmith – for introducing me to "Fred" and providing insights into more life and love-transforming tools.
- Abby Kunnecke – for the hours upon hours of support via delicious food, conversations over tea, taking Aavi out on walks, and providing your expert reader opinions.
- My incredible network of support – especially those around the globe who took the time to share their opinion on cover design and book title!
- My amazing clients – through years of working with you, I have grown so much both personally and professionally. Thank you for sharing your stories, vulnerability, and passions. I am honored to work with each of you.
- Tricia Hagen – for years of support and wise counsel through so many stages of life. You are a wise soul, and I am blessed to have you in my life.
- Peer Editors: Jaymin Patel, Charlie Glickman, Kathy Labriola, Sarah Jones, Abby Kunnecke, Karen Pizzuto Sharp, Tyler Wagner, Sara Dwyer, Jordan Giarratano, Rhena-Dae Cwiek, Hunter Riley, Melissa Mango, Natalie, Vartanian, Chris Lye, Allena Gabosch, Liz Joynt Sandberg, Kathleen Ashford, Pete Mosq, Robyn Klopp, Rachel Bowen, Yoni Alkan, Sebastian Gaertner, Briana Jacobs, Gabrielle Knight, Koe Creation, Sarah Burgart, Sarah Schneider, and Taralynn Carter – thank you all for investing your time into sharing feedback on this book! I am so grateful for your thoughts and suggestions.

About the Contributing Author

 **Adam Kardos** lives in Seattle, Washington. He's a Voice Actor, Tech Fairy, and has actively participated in discussion, mediation, and fostering of alternative lifestyles over the last 8 years. Adam trained in Life Coaching with New Ventures West in San Francisco, California, and is a lifelong student of human discovery.

About the Author

 **Eri Kardos** is an international speaker and relationship coach. She specializes in empowering people to choose their own adventure in relationships, career, and life. Prior to studying in San Francisco and Copenhagen to earn her certification as an Integral Coach, Eri graduated from the world's #1 international business school and provided leadership within the tech industry. Having provided game-changing relationship coaching to top leaders at companies including Amazon, Google, and Microsoft, Eri now works with clients all over the world to help them fall more deeply in love with their partners, themselves, and their relationships.

Are you ready to be empowered for your next adventure?
Eri has delivered hundreds of self-development presentations, workshops, unconferences, and private coaching sessions across the globe. She regularly partners with corporations, universities, business groups, and community organizations.

She is known for her passion and insight on a wide variety of Personal and Relationship Development topics including building a new relationship foundation, preparing for marriage (and other big commitments), allowing individuals and relationships to grow over time, getting "unstuck" when a relationship has stagnated, building more intimacy, making a clear co-parenting plan, creating smoother transitions when a relationship is ending, opening a safer space for divorce and other potentially difficult conversations, and fostering a friendship based on mutual understanding after the romance is gone.

She provides private video and phone coaching sessions to clients around the world. In addition, she offers in-person facilitated retreats and fully guided intensives to help individuals and couples create the relationships and life they desire.

Connect with Eri:
www.EriKardos.com
LinkedIn (Eri Kardos), Twitter (@Eri_Kardos),
Facebook (www.facebook.com/EriKardosCoaching)

A Final Note:
Is This Book Written for You?

Is this book really written for you? If you already have your ideal relationship where you and your partner have solid communication, navigate conflict like pros, explore profound intimacy, and flow easily through life's changes together, then you are already living what most couples dream of! I can assure you that the tools and tips in *Relationship Agreements* will complement the partnership you already have and add new depth as you continue to grow together.

However, if you are like most people, you are either seeking your ideal partnership or you desire something more in the one you are choosing to be in right now. In this case, just by picking up this guide, you are already ahead of much of the population because you are making the choice to step into designing the relationship and life that you desire!

I personally wish I had an approach and a book like this when I began my journey into dating and partnerships. Instead, I read hundreds of books, attended dozens of workshops, talked with friends and family for countless hours into the night about lessons they learned, had my own fair share of growth experiences, and worked with some of the best coaches to gain the insights summarized in this book. It contains everything you need to identify, articulate, and explore all the aspects of your relationship to make it what you want. I've spent hours creating and perfecting the invitations (homework) at the end of each chapter. I have used each one with numerous clients all over the globe and have seen bigger breakthroughs happen in their relationships than they had ever imagined.

If you're like the wonderful people I've had the honor of coaching, you are capable and willing to do the work to achieve the changes you desire in your current situation. I wrote this book with you in mind. Also, much like my clients, you might have limited bandwidth in terms of time, ability, or just mindshare to break through to the "next level" on your own. If this sounds like you, I invite you to connect with me, and I'd be happy to guide you to the results you seek as I've done for so many clients all over the globe. Relationships are at the foundation of all success, often providing fuel for us to shine in all other areas of our life – career, money, community, family, spirit, and so on.

Your success is important to me – that's why I wrote this book: to help people fall more deeply in love with their partner, themselves, and their relationship. You can choose the approach that works best for you and your relationship. Here are a few ways I can support you in getting what you desire:

- Work with me as a couple or as an individual via private video coaching from anywhere in the world, and we can move toward your ideal relationship (and life!).
- Attend one of my "made for you" destination retreats for couples who want to take charge of their relationship in a fun and relaxed setting. I take care of all the details, and you walk away with your new Relationship Agreement in hand and a fun vacation in a sexy destination!
- Partner with me for a 5-hour intensive coaching session where you (and your partner) will uncover your patterns, establish a clear path forward, get a fast download of incredible relationship tools, and co-create your own "done-for-you" Relationship Agreements to transform your current situation to one that you both have designed! (Recommended for couples who want a fast-track change!)

Utilize this book as your relationship guide, and I look forward to connecting with you and investing in the success of your relationship!

Made in the USA
Monee, IL
26 April 2021